W9-BUM-602

CC17

THE DECADES OF TWENTIETH-CENTURY AMERICA

AMERICA IN THE 1950s

EDMUND LINDOP with
SARAH DECAPUA

Twenty-First Century Books · Minneapolis

Twenty-First Century Books
A division of Lerner Publishing Group, Inc.
241 First Avenue North
Minneapolis, MN 55401 U.S.A.

Website address: www.lernerbooks.com

Library of Congress Cataloging-in-Publication Data

Lindop, Edmund.
    America in the 1950s / by Edmund Lindop with Sarah DeCapua.
        p.   cm. – (The decades of twentieth-century America)
    Includes bibliographical references and index.
    ISBN 978–0–8225–7642–6 (lib. bdg. : alk. paper)
        1. United States—Civilization—1945– —Juvenile literature. 2. United
States—History—1945–1953—Juvenile literature. 3. United States—
History—1953–1961—Juvenile literature. 4. Nineteen fifties—Juvenile
literature. I. DeCapua, Sarah. II. Title. III. Title: America in the nineteen
fifties.
    E169.12.L546 2010
    973.92—dc22   2008040127

Manufactured in the United States of America
1 2 3 4 5 6 – VI – 15 14 13 12 11 10

CONTENTS ★★★★★★★★★★★★★★

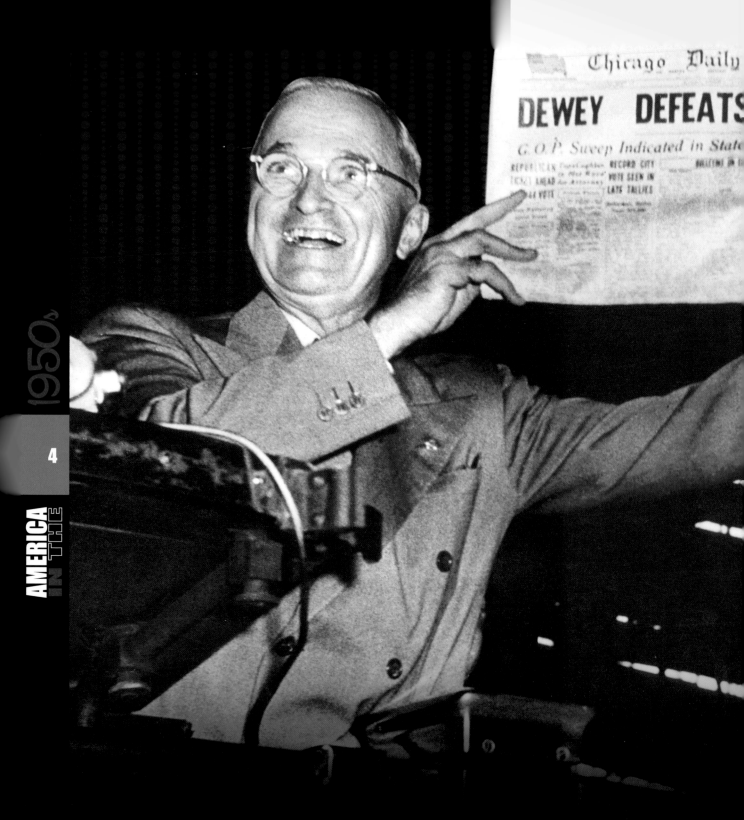

As the new decade began, HARRY TRUMAN sat in the White House. His victory in the 1948 presidential election is considered one of the most shocking political upsets in U.S. history. Truman's opponent, Thomas Dewey, was so far ahead in the polls that the *Chicago Daily Tribune*

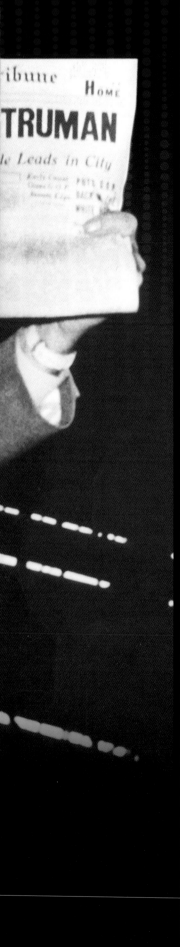

FROM WAR TO PEACE TO WAR

The 1950s were one of the most significant decades in the history of the United States. Sandwiched between two decades of war—World War II in the 1940s and the Vietnam War in the 1960s—the 1950s are sometimes seen as the decade of fun and frolic. While this is partly true, the decade also saw its own war—the Korean War—as well as important technological and economic advances. For example, the "space race" of that era not only led to the nation's first moon landing (1969) and satellites in space but also to remarkable new developments in computer technology and medicine.

The development of the hydrogen bomb in the 1950s accelerated the tension between the United States and the Soviet Union (a nation in Eastern Europe and northern and central Asia that formed in 1922 and split into several republics in 1991). The conflict between the United States and the Soviet Union over economic, ideological (political), and governmental differences became known as the Cold War (1945–1991). The Cold War never developed into armed conflict between the two nations. But tensions and competition between the two countries were fierce until the breakup of the Soviet Union in the 1990s.

Vast changes in American lifestyles sprang from the advent of television, the movement of people from cities to suburbs, and increased economic productivity. Equally important was the extension of civil rights to minorities, especially black Americans.

■ A PROMISING FUTURE

From 1941 to 1945, Americans endured the devastating effects of World War II (1939–1945). When the war ended, people throughout the world celebrated. The war cost millions of lives, left other millions permanently injured, and destroyed huge amounts of property. The Allies, consisting of the United States, Great Britain, France, and the Soviet Union, had conquered Adolf Hitler's Germany, Benito Mussolini's Italy, and the warlords of imperial Japan.

The prospects for a lasting peace appeared bright. To help preserve this peace, the United Nations (UN) was established in 1945. It replaced the League of Nations, which had been established at the end of World War I (1914–1918). UN members included most of the world's nations, including the Allied nations of World War II.

After the war, the United States hastily disbanded most of its armed forces. Millions of American men and women were freed from military duty and returned to their families. "No people in history have been known to disengage themselves so quickly from the ways of war," commented President Harry S. Truman. By early 1947, U.S. armed forces had been cut from their wartime strength of 12 million to 1.5 million. The annual military budget had dropped from $90.9 billion to $10.3 billion.

THOUSANDS OF PEOPLE CROWD INTO NEW YORK CITY'S TIMES SQUARE TO CELEBRATE THE ANNOUNCEMENT OF JAPAN'S SURRENDER on August 15, 1945, which ended World War II.

■ A FORMER ALLY TURNS CHALLENGER

The Soviet Union—a U.S. ally in World War II—did not dismantle its war machine, however. It kept its huge army, military airplanes, and a large fleet of fighting ships. With these resources, the Soviets planned to extend their system of government—Communism—over vast areas. Communism is a way of organizing a country's economy so that, in theory, all citizens benefit equally from a nation's wealth. To achieve this goal, the government controls all decisions about land, housing, factories, and businesses. Profits are distributed among all the citizens. This generally means that citizens give up privacy and other personal freedoms. In contrast, the United States has a mostly capitalist system. In capitalism most of the land, housing, factories, and businesses belong to private individuals rather than to the government. Citizens are responsible for creating their own wealth and enjoy a range of personal freedoms.

Even before World War II ended, the Soviet Union had taken over three small independent countries on the Baltic Sea—Estonia, Latvia, and Lithuania. Following the war, it broke its promise to permit free elections in Poland and other countries in Eastern Europe. Instead, it gained control of these nations, which then became Communist states. These countries were known as "puppet" states because they were controlled by government leaders in faraway Moscow, the Soviet Union's capital. In 1946 former British prime minister Winston Churchill solemnly declared that an "Iron Curtain has descended" to cut off from the world these Soviet-controlled countries in Eastern Europe. The term

This political cartoon of Winston Churchill peaking under the iron curtain was created shortly after he gave what is known as the **"IRON CURTAIN" SPEECH**.

iron curtain would come into widespread use throughout the world until the 1991 breakup of the Soviet Union.

When the Soviet Union attempted to extend its rule into Greece and Turkey in 1947, U.S. president Harry S. Truman and the U.S. Congress quickly furnished military and economic assistance that prevented a Communist takeover of those countries. Also in 1947, the United States launched the Marshall Plan, which was intended to help Europe recover economically from the ravages of World War II. The plan provided $13 billion in loans to sixteen European countries. (The Soviet Union was offered a chance to participate in this plan, but it turned down U.S. assistance.)

■ A DIVIDED GERMANY

After the war, defeated Germany was divided into four zones. The victors of the war—the United States, Great Britain, France, and the Soviet Union—each were assigned control of one zone until a peace treaty could be signed to reunite Germany. The Soviets, however, refused to permit their zone to be merged with the other zones. Consequently, Germany remained divided and eventually became two separate nations—democratic West Germany and Communist East Germany. (The two countries were reunited under democratic rule in 1990.)

Berlin, Germany's largest city, lay 110 miles (177 kilometers) inside East Germany. It was divided into two sections, Communist East Berlin and democratic West Berlin. In 1948 Communist leaders shut down all the highways, railroads, and water routes that ran from West Berlin to West Germany. By cutting off all vital trade links between isolated West Berlin and West Germany, the Communists gambled that West Berliners would be forced to give in to Communist rule.

President Truman, however, was determined to keep West Berlin from being absorbed by the Communists. In June 1948, he ordered a massive airlift in which large numbers of airplanes flew food, fuel, and other supplies to West Berlin. This was a dangerous move, since the Communists might have attacked the planes, perhaps starting World War III. But the Communists did not interfere with the flights, and many months later, they ended their siege of West Berlin.

West Berliners watch as a U.S. Air Force plane arrives. Part of the **BERLIN AIRLIFT OF 1948**, the plane brought supplies to the blockaded city.

■ INTERNATIONAL DEVELOPMENTS

In 1949 the North Atlantic Treaty Organization (NATO) was formed. It provided a military alliance among various European nations and the United States. NATO members pledged joint action in the event of Communist attack against any member nation. The United States took the lead in proposing NATO, and U.S. general Dwight D. Eisenhower (a hero of World War II) was its first military commander.

In 1949, after a lengthy civil war, Chinese Communist forces headed by Mao Zedong conquered China's non-Communist government, led by Chiang Kai-shek. Chiang's followers were forced to flee to the island of Formosa (present-day Taiwan). China then became a Communist ally of the Soviet Union.

Despite the deteriorating relations between the free world and the Communist powers, most Americans felt reasonably secure because they alone had atomic bombs. They believed no country would dare attack the United States or its allies and risk possible annihilation (total destruction). Then, on September 23, 1949, President Truman grimly announced that the Soviet Union had exploded an atomic device. This shocking revelation instantly and dramatically altered the perception of a permanent global peace.

A national poll in 1950 showed that 41 percent of Americans believed their country would fight another war within five years. Seventy-five percent believed that Communists would drop atomic bombs on U.S. cities in the next war. Nineteen percent feared that another war would destroy the entire human race. Only five years after World War II ended, the Cold War had taken center stage. It would frighten people throughout the world for nearly half a century.

A landing ship, tank (LST) carrying a regiment of U.S. TROOPS LANDS AT INCHON HARBOR, KOREA, IN 1950.

Chapter One

NEW DECADE, NEW CONFLICT:

The Korean War

During the final weeks of World War II, both U.S. and Soviet troops moved to occupy the Asian nation of Korea, which had been annexed (absorbed) by Japan in 1910. Americans held the southern part of this peninsula east of China. The Soviets took over the northern part. This division followed an agreement that came out of the Yalta Conference in 1945. The agreement permitted Soviet and U.S. armed forces to occupy Korea. A line to divide the two sections of Korea was established along the thirty-eighth parallel of latitude. This temporary division was to last until the establishment of a unified and independent Korean government.

The plan to establish a united Korea was unsuccessful. The Soviet Union blocked UN attempts to hold elections to create a unified state. As a result, a Communist government was established in North Korea and a democratic government was set up in South Korea.

At first, the United States showed little interest in defending South Korea against possible aggression from North Korea. In June 1949, U.S. troops were removed from South Korea. Then, in January 1950, U.S. secretary of state Dean Acheson announced a new U.S. policy in Asia. The United States would protect an area that ran from the Aleutian Islands (off the coast of Alaska) south across the Pacific Ocean to Japan and the Philippines. But

11

any aggression occurring outside this area and where Korea was located was to be dealt with by the parties involved or by the UN.

■ NORTH KOREA INVADES SOUTH KOREA

On June 25, 1950, at 9:26 A.M., the U.S. State Department received a startling telegram from John Muccio, the U.S. ambassador in South Korea. It read: "North Korean forces invaded [South] Korea at several places this morning. . . . It would appear from the nature of the attack and the manner in which it was launched that it constitutes an all-out [war] against [South] Korea."

" North Korean forces invaded [South] Korea at several places this morning."

—*U.S. ambassador John Muccio, in a telegram to President Truman, June 25, 1950*

President Truman knew that the South Koreans were facing an aggressor with an enormous advantage. North Korea's armed forces totaled 150,000. Although the Soviets had removed their troops from North Korea, they had left behind a large amount of equipment, including guns, weapons, tanks, and military airplanes.

Against this formidable foe, the South Koreans had only sixty-five thousand troops. Only a small number of troops were stationed near the border to defend the country. South Koreans were poorly armed, with outdated weapons and supplies.

When Trygve Lie, the first secretary-general of the UN, heard about the invasion, he declared, "This is war against the United States." And so it was. The two Koreas were members of the UN, and the United States represented the UN in South Korea.

Members of the UN Security Council (a small group of the world's most powerful nations, including the United States and the Soviet Union) hastily assembled in an emergency meeting. They voted that the UN would take up arms to end North Korean aggression. The North Korean government did not respond to the UN resolution. So two days later, a follow-up resolution provided that

THE UN SECURITY COUNCIL VOTES ON RESPONDING TO NORTH KOREAN AGGRESSION
during an emergency session on June 25, 1950. The Soviet Union's representative did not attend.

"the members of the United Nations furnish such assistance to [South Korea] as may be necessary to repel the armed attack and to restore international peace and security in the area." The Security Council designated the United States as the lead country in pursuing the war in Korea.

Besides the United States, fifteen other nations sent military forces to South Korea, eventually numbering about nineteen thousand troops. Forty-one other countries sent money, food, clothing, and medical supplies. Troops from the United States and South Korea did most of the fighting.

President Truman named General Douglas MacArthur as commander of the UN armed forces in Korea. During World War II, MacArthur had led the U.S. campaign in the Pacific Ocean. General MacArthur faced a difficult task in defending South Korea. The fast-moving North Koreans nearly won the war in its first few weeks. They captured the South Korean capital of Seoul and quickly pressed forward until they almost reached the port of Pusan, at the southern tip of the peninsula.

On September 15, 1950, U.S. Marines successfully assaulted Inchon, a South Korean port city west of Seoul. They were followed by a large contingent of army troops. Two weeks later, Seoul fell. By October 1, the UN

Harry S. Truman was the thirty-third president of the United States, serving from 1945 until 1953. Truman was born in Missouri on May 8, 1884. He served with U.S. forces during World War I, which began in Europe in 1914. When the war ended in 1918, he returned to Missouri and married Elizabeth (Bess) Wallace. He was elected a county judge in 1922 and, in 1934, a U.S. senator. He was named President Franklin D. Roosevelt's running mate in 1944 and was elected vice president later that year.

Just three months after his inauguration as vice president, Truman became president in April 1945, following Roosevelt's death. Truman spent the remainder of the term focusing on the rebuilding of war-torn Europe, advancing civil rights in the United States, and containing the spread of Communism in the world. Truman went on to win his own term as president (1949–1953)

PRESIDENT HARRY S. TRUMAN signs a proclamation in the White House in 1950.

over heavily favored Thomas E. Dewey in one of the most stunning victories in U.S. political history. After his presidency, Truman retired to his Missouri home, where he died on December 26, 1972.

forces held a line near the thirty-eighth parallel. Under heavy fire, the North Korean soldiers retreated into their own country. South Korea again was a free and independent nation.

■ THE UN COUNTERATTACK PROVOKES A DANGEROUS NEW FOE

Americans wondered what would happen next. Would the UN forces be content with having liberated South Korea? Or would they move north of the thirty-eighth parallel and try to unify the two Koreas?

At first, President Truman told the American people that the U.S. National Security Council had studied the matter and recommended against crossing the thirty-eighth parallel. General MacArthur, however, insisted that his troops be permitted to invade the North. If this happened, he predicted that all of Korea would be united by Thanksgiving.

The UN General Assembly (including all UN member nations) passed a resolution calling for the unification of Korea. This gave MacArthur the authority he needed to send his forces northward. The Chinese foreign minister then issued a statement that said if the UN armies crossed the thirty-eighth parallel, "China would send troops to the Korean frontier to defend North Korea." MacArthur did not believe the Chinese.

UN forces pushed triumphantly through most of North Korea. Its capital, Pyongyang, and the east coast port of Wonsan were captured easily in October 1950. Just as it appeared that North Korean resistance had completely collapsed, U.S. troops advancing ahead of UN forces encountered huge Chinese units just south of the border between China and North Korea. By November 2, there was clear evidence that China had massed about 850,000 troops on the border.

U.S. TROOPS ARE HUNKERED DOWN in North Korea in late 1950. Communist Chinese troops joined North Korea's fight after UN forces crossed the thirty-eighth parallel, which had divided North Korea and South Korea.

As thousands of Chinese soldiers stormed into North Korea, a disaster of huge proportions began taking shape. The U.S. Second Infantry Division tried desperately to halt the Chinese advance. But in the final few days of November, the Second Division suffered five thousand casualties, or roughly one-third of its men.

On November 30, the UN forces were swiftly retreating. At a White House press conference that same day, a reporter asked President Truman whether he might use the atomic bomb to end the war. The president replied, "There has always been active consideration of its use." Truman knew that such action would trigger World War III, which he strongly wanted to avoid.

The Chinese armies were strengthened by additional North Korean troops. The combined troops continued to push southward. Finally, they reached the thirty-eighth parallel, where the war had begun.

■ A STALEMATE LEADS TO PEACE

Truman replaced MacArthur as commander of the UN forces in Korea in April 1951. U.S. general Matthew Ridgway took over. By mid-June, the UN forces had stopped the North Korean advance near the thirty-eighth parallel. A short time later, the Chinese and North Koreans agreed to meet UN representatives at a town called Panmunjom to begin negotiating a peace treaty. But the negotiations dragged on for months. Meanwhile, sporadic fighting continued.

North Korean *(left)* and UN *(right)* representatives meet at **PANMUNJOM IN 1951 TO DISCUSS A CEASE-FIRE.**

DOUGLAS MACARTHUR rides in a ticker-tape parade through New York after returning from Korea in 1951.

General Douglas MacArthur firmly believed that there was no "substitute for victory" in the Korean War. To accomplish this goal, his plan was to bomb military and industrial sites in China, set up a naval blockade of China's coasts, and allow anti-Communist troops in Formosa (modern Taiwan) to invade the Chinese mainland.

President Truman disagreed with MacArthur. Truman wanted to limit the war in Korea because he hoped that would preserve the lives of U.S. troops. He was also desperate to avoid a third world war. Because of this profound disagreement, Truman officially fired the general on April 11, 1951. The general's dismissal unleashed one of the hottest controversies of the decade.

Truman's supporters thought he had acted correctly as the nation's commander in chief. But his critics believed MacArthur's firing would embolden the Communists to attack other countries. In spite of these differences, ordinary Americans remembered MacArthur's honorable service in both world wars. Huge crowds hailed him as a hero when he returned to the United States on April 17, 1951. In San Francisco, California, thousands of enthusiastic supporters lined the streets to catch a glimpse of the general as he traveled from the airport to a hotel. A trip that should have taken only a few minutes took two hours.

Two days later, MacArthur delivered a speech to Congress, which an estimated 20 million people watched on television. He maintained that the free world could not surrender to Communists in Asia. His concluding remarks were so dramatic that they were remembered for decades by the people who heard them: "I still remember the refrain of [a popular military ballad] which proclaimed most proudly that old soldiers never die; they just fade away. And like the old soldier of that ballad, I now close my military career and just fade away, an old soldier who tried to do his duty as God gave him the light to see that duty. Good-bye."

MacArthur remained a hero to countless Americans. He lived quietly in New York for the remainder of his life. Millions around the world mourned his death in 1964. Historian David McCullough later observed, "There's no question . . . about his importance as one of the [major figures] of the twentieth century."

North Korean and Chinese Communist soldiers sit in a **UN PRISONER-OF-WAR CAMP IN 1951.**

The most difficult issue to resolve at the negotiating table was what to do about prisoners of war (POWs) on both sides. At first, Communist leaders insisted on forced repatriation (obligatory return to a prisoner's home country). But many Communist prisoners did not want to return home. Aid workers with the International Red Cross polled the POWs. The results were announced in April 1952. The poll showed that of 132,000 Chinese and North Korean prisoners, only 54,000 North Koreans and 5,100 Chinese wanted to be sent home. It was a staggering blow to Communist pride and greatly stalled the negotiations.

A year passed before a solution to the POW problem was established. A neutral commission interviewed the prisoners. If they did not want to go back home, the commission would allow them to be released to whatever country they chose.

On July 27, 1953, the peace treaty was finally signed with no clear winner. The human losses in the Korean War were enormous. Chinese and North Korean casualties were not announced, but estimates of their total losses amounted to nearly two million military troops, plus about another 1 million civilians (people who are not in the military). Total casualties (killed, wounded, and missing) for the UN forces were 459,300, of whom more than 250,000 were South Koreans. Of the 1.8 million Americans who served in Korea, 54,200 were killed, 103,300 were wounded, and 8,200 were labeled as missing in action (MIA).

While neither side was fully victorious in the Korean War, the conflict had allowed the United States to keep its military forces combat-ready. In addition, the Korean hostilities prompted the United States to strengthen its military commitment to NATO. And in 1954, the Southeast Asia Treaty Organization (SEATO) was created to provide unified defense if member nations in Southeast Asia were attacked.

The Korean War also saw the end of U.S. discrimination against black soldiers. During World War I and World War II, African Americans had fought in segregated (separated according to race) divisions. In 1948 President Truman ordered the armed forces to be integrated (no longer separated according to race). During the Korean War, black and white service people fought side by side, ate in the same mess halls, and slept in the same barracks.

U.S. SOLDIERS FOUGHT IN INTEGRATED UNITS in the Korean War.

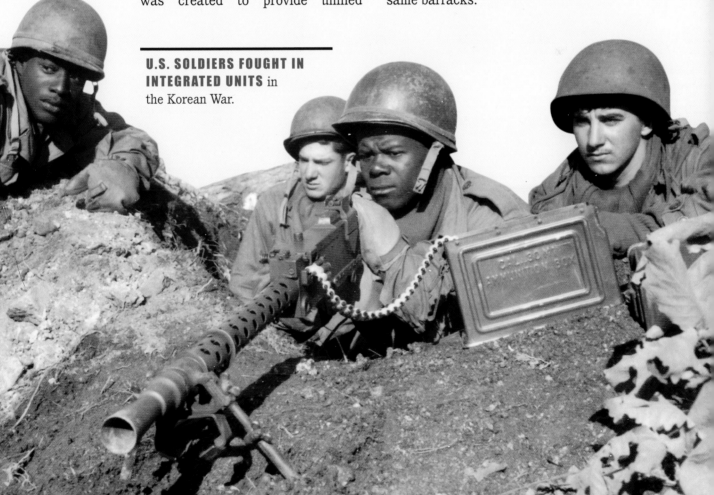

SENATOR JOSEPH MCCARTHY testifies during a 1954 hearing before the U.S. House of Representatives. The map behind him shows his assessment of Communist activity in the United States.

Chapter Two

"BETTER DEAD THAN RED":

The Red Scare and the Cold War

Recalling President Truman's 1949 announcement that the Soviet Union had exploded an atomic weapon, many Americans wondered how the Soviets could have acquired the technology so soon after World War II. People wondered if widespread espionage (spying) on behalf of the Soviets had made their achievement possible.

The nation was gripped by fear. "Better dead than Red," an anti-Communist slogan that may have first been used during World War II, came into widespread use. (Anything related to a Communist country, especially the Soviet Union, was referred to as Red.) In response to the nation's unease, President Truman launched a massive security program in 1947. Between 1947 and 1952, about 6.6 million government employees were investigated. Not a single case of espionage was uncovered, but about 500 people were fired from their jobs because of "questionable loyalty." Despite the failure to find spies, this "Red Hunt" led many Americans to fear that the government was riddled with spies. Yet other Americans thought that the U.S. government was going too far in its efforts to uncover Communists. They viewed these efforts as witch hunts, in which many innocent people were investigated for no reason.

The U.S. House of Representatives had formed the House Un-American Activities Committee (HUAC) in 1938. Members of the committee investigated alleged disloyalty and antigovernment activities on the part of private citizens, public officials, and people and organizations suspected of having Communist ties. Richard M. Nixon, a California congressman (and later U.S. president), became a national hero to some as the leader of this committee. During the 1950s, the committee's meetings were broadcast on television to millions of viewers across the country. Americans suspected of pro-Communist activities—sometimes on flimsy evidence, if any—were questioned by the committee. For example, Alger Hiss, a former State Department official who had helped establish the UN, was questioned. Whittaker Chambers, a self-confessed former Communist spy, claimed that in the 1930s, Hiss had given him secret government documents. Chambers turned over these documents to the HUAC, but Hiss strongly denied his involvement.

On January 21, 1950, Hiss was convicted of perjury (lying under oath)—though not of espionage—following two highly publicized trials. His conviction led to a five-year prison sentence. Nixon declared at that time that it was only "a small part of the whole shocking story of Communist espionage in the United States."

Two weeks after Hiss was found guilty, the British government an-

During the 1950s, the committee's meetings were broadcast on television to millions of viewers across the country. Americans suspected of pro-Communist activities—sometimes on flimsy evidence, if any—were questioned by the committee.

nounced the arrest of Dr. Klaus Fuchs, a scientist who had worked on the development of the atomic bomb at Los Alamos, New Mexico, during World War II. Fuchs confessed to having spied for the Soviet Union and to giving that country top-secret information on how to build the bomb.

Investigators linked Fuchs to American Communists Harry Gold, Morton Sobel, and Julius and Ethel Rosenberg. Gold and Sobel were convicted of espionage and given long prison terms. When the Federal Bureau of Investigation (FBI) questioned Julius Rosenberg, he refused to answer. At the Rosenbergs' trial, both repeatedly invoked the U.S. Constitution's Fifth Amendment. The Fifth Amendment protects an individual's right not to say anything that would indicate that he or she is guilty.

The story of Julius and Ethel Rosenberg riveted and divided Americans for decades. On one side were people who believed that the Rosenbergs were guilty and that their execution was just. On the other side were those who claimed the Rosenbergs were victims of anti-Semitism (dislike of Jews) and of a hostile government that wanted to stir up fear and hatred among ordinary Americans. They claimed that the Rosenbergs were executed not for spying but for merely being Communists, an unpopular position at the height of the Cold War.

In September 2008, however, the argument was decisively ended when Morton Sobel, the Rosenbergs' codefendant, admitted that he and Julius had indeed been spies for the Soviet Union. Sobel's confession, at the age of ninety-one, stunned many who had believed Sobel and the Rosenbergs were innocent. Since his conviction in 1953, Sobel, too, had denied that he had been a spy. But Sobel confirmed that he and the Rosenbergs began working against the United States in 1942. They passed along to the Soviets top-secret information about the U.S. atomic program, as well as information on U.S. radar and sonar. That information may have been used to create weapons that shot down U.S. planes in the Korean and Vietnam wars. Sobel's confes-

These photos of JULIUS AND ETHEL ROSENBERG were taken shortly after their arrest in 1950.

sion of these serious crimes against the United States put to rest the controversy surrounding the Rosenbergs.

Also in September 2008, documents were unsealed indicating that while a large portion of the evidence pointed toward Ethel Rosenberg's guilt, some of the testimony used to convict her was made up. This means that while she was proven guilty, her execution was likely a miscarriage of justice.

The jury saw this behavior as an indication of the Rosenbergs' guilt. The jury convicted them of espionage, and they were sentenced to death by electric chair. The execution took place on June 19, 1953. The Rosenbergs, who had two young sons, were the first native-born Americans to be put to death for espionage by order of a civilian court. The case remained controversial for decades. In 2008 Sobel admitted publicly that he and the Rosenbergs were indeed guilty.

■ REDS UNDER THE BEDS

One evening in 1950, a couple in Houston, Texas, entered a Chinese restaurant and talked with the owner about producing a radio program about recent Chinese history. Overhearing their conversation, a nearby customer phoned the police and told them that the people were "talking Communism." The couple were arrested and questioned for fourteen hours before the police concluded that there was no evidence of espionage.

Such behavior was common during this period of fear of Communism known as the Red Scare. In a 1954 national survey, more than half of the respondents said that all known Communists should be jailed. Seventy-eight percent thought Americans should report to the FBI neighbors or acquaintances whom they suspected of being Communists.

Many states, cities, and counties imposed loyalty oaths on teachers and college professors. So did some corporations and labor unions. These workers had to swear their allegiance to the United States and affirm that they had never had any Communist ties.

About 250 Hollywood personalities were blacklisted (denied jobs) during the early 1950s because they were either suspected of having or known to have had Communist ties. This blacklisting also spread to Broadway and to the music industry. Among the best-known blacklisted individuals were actors Jose Ferrer, Will Geer, Lee J. Cobb, Edward G. Robinson, and actor-director Orson Welles; writers Arthur Miller, Lillian Hellman, Dashiell Hammett, Langston Hughes, and Ring Lardner Jr.; singers Paul Robeson, Lena Horne, and Pete Seeger; composer Aaron Copland; and composer-conductor Leonard Bernstein. For example, Miller and Hellman were accused of writing plays that contained "subversive" ideas, or ideas that supported Communism. Robeson was charged with having Communist contacts.

The blacklist ruined the professional lives of many artists. Some were unable to find work in the United States for many years. As a result, a few moved overseas. One blacklisted writer, Dalton Trumbo, used the pseudonym (fake name) Robert Rich to write a screenplay for which he won an Academy Award in 1956.

The media rushed to turn out tales with strongly anti-Communist themes. Hollywood produced films such as *I Married a Communist*, *The Iron Curtain*, *The Red Menace*, and *I Was a Communist for the FBI*. Bookstores carried titles such as *The Red Plotters*, *The Soviet Spies*, and *I Chose Freedom*. Herbert Philbrick's story about how he had been a Communist and then an FBI informant, *I Led Three Lives*, was serialized in several installments in about five hundred U.S. newspapers and adapted into a television series.

HOLLYWOOD SCREENWRITER DALTON TRUMBO *(center)*, an American Communist, refused to cooperate with the HUAC. He was soon banned from working in the movie industry. Yet Trumbo continued to write movie scripts under a false name.

■ THE RED SCARE AND EVERYDAY AMERICANS

The Red Scare affected Americans in other ways. Many people feared deadly nuclear bomb attacks could occur at any time. In public schools during the fifties, students participated in drills designed to protect them from falling bombs. When the teacher spoke the signal word *drop*, they jumped from their seats and scurried beneath desks and tables, where they shielded their heads under their arms. Or they filed from their classrooms into school hallways and stood with their backs against the walls.

Some families were so frightened by the possibility of nuclear destruction that they hired companies to build expensive underground concrete shelters with steel tops and stairs to the bottom in their backyards. They equipped the shelters with a radio, batteries, supplies of water and canned foods, and games and toys for the children. Anxious neighbors often asked the shelter owners if they had room for their families too.

MANY FAMILIES OF THE 1950s BUILT OR PURCHASED THEIR OWN NUCLEAR FALLOUT SHELTERS. They stocked them with about two weeks' worth of food, water, and supplies.

■ MCCARTHY CRUSADES AGAINST COMMUNISTS

Joseph McCarthy was elected a U.S. senator from Wisconsin in 1946. He became a major voice in the campaign to expose Communists in the United States. He was eager to pursue those in the government, which he claimed was "full of Communists."

McCarthy first drew national attention with a sensational speech before a women's club in Wheeling, West Virginia, on February 9, 1950. "I have here in my hand," he declared, waving a sheaf of papers, "a list of 205 names known to the secretary of state as being members of the Communist Party and who nevertheless are still working and shaping the policy of the State Department." The senator told the club that he thought the United States was in a weak position in international affairs "not because our only powerful potential enemy has sent men to invade our shores, but rather because of the traitorous actions of those who have been treated so well by this Nation."

> **"I have here in my hand a list of 205 names known to the secretary of state as being members of the Communist Party and who nevertheless are still working and shaping the policy of the State Department."**

—*Senator Joseph McCarthy, speech to the Wheeling (West Virginia) Women's Club, February 9, 1950*

When later asked to produce his list of 205 Communists in the State Department, McCarthy would not produce it. In a subsequent speech, he reduced the number to 57 but again did not identify any of those whom he accused.

Finally, McCarthy began to name some of his targets. They included U.S. secretary of state Dean Acheson and Philip Jessup, the U.S. ambassador to the United Nations. McCarthy also accused a top general in the U.S. armed forces of being a Communist. Despite the lack of concrete evidence against those he accused, McCarthy had many supporters who approved of his campaign against U.S. Communists. A national poll conducted on May 21, 1950, showed that 46.4 percent of Americans thought McCarthy was doing "a good thing for the country." More than 34 percent thought he was not, and 19 percent had no opinion.

Over time, McCarthy's campaign became increasingly zealous, and the nation tired of his accusations. Four years after McCarthy began his crusade to root out Communists, the U.S. Senate voted to censure (reprimand) him on December 2, 1954. The term "McCarthyism" came into widespread use. For some, it described the leading figure of the anti-Communist movement. For others, it pointed to the senator's aggressive style of rooting out Communists in the U.S. government and society.

■ THE COLD WAR

In August 1945, the United States dropped atomic bombs on the Japanese cities of Hiroshima and Nagasaki, bringing World War II to an end. As a result of the devastation and tremendous loss of life, some of the scientists who had helped develop the atomic bomb opposed the idea of building an even deadlier bomb. For example, Albert Einstein expressed his worries in 1950, when he observed that "radioactive poisoning of the atmosphere and hence annihilation of any life on earth has been brought within the range of technical possibilities."

Still, other people saw important reasons for developing a bomb that was more powerful than the atomic bomb. During the Cold War years, many Americans were concerned about the eagerness of the Soviet Union to expand its control globally. In addition, the Soviets had a much larger army than those of the United States and its allies. But the most important reason was the awful possibility that the Soviet Union would build the superbomb first.

"I don't think you have a choice," Rear Admiral Sidney Souers of the National Security Council told President Truman. "It's either we make it or wait until the Russians drop one on us without warning." On January 31, 1950, President Truman decided that work on the hydrogen bomb would begin.

■ A TORRENT OF DEVASTATING WEAPONS

The atomic bomb is based on nuclear fission. This means the nucleus of an atom is split, which releases large amounts of energy. The hydrogen bomb (H-bomb) is based on nuclear fusion, or bringing together atoms of hydrogen—the same element that fuels the sun—to release energy. The heat at the center of this superbomb is at least five times greater than that at the interior of the sun. And it has the explosive force of 5 million tons (4.5 metric tons) of TNT (an explosive compound made up of carbon, hydrogen, nitrogen, and oxygen).

On November 1, 1952, the first test of the H-bomb took place at Eniwetok, an atoll (a chain of tiny coral islands that forms a ring around a lagoon) in the Pacific Ocean. The bomb's power surprised even the scientists who observed it from planes and ships 50 miles (80 km) away. Its nuclear matter rose like a gigantic cloud about 25 miles (40 km) into the atmosphere and spread 100 miles (161 km) across the sky. The H-bomb gouged out such a huge crater that Eniwetok disappeared.

When news of the H-bomb was released, people throughout the world were terrified. They understood that a weapon that could destroy all civilization had been created. In addition to wiping out cities, its radioactivity had the power to end all forms of life on Earth. Americans hoped that the Soviet Union would not be able to develop the same weapon. But their fears were realized when the Soviets exploded an H-bomb in Siberia in 1953, just nine months after the U.S. test. The arms race was on.

U.S. Strategic Air Command jets patrolled the skies day and night. The navy constructed carriers large enough to carry nuclear bombs. In 1954 the navy launched the *Nautilus*, the first atomic-powered submarine. It had the ability to shoot nuclear weapons while submerged.

A mushroom cloud rises over Eniwetok after **U.S. SCIENTISTS EXPLODED THE FIRST H-BOMB** on the small Pacific atoll in 1952.

1950s

30

AMERICA IN THE

The space race was another type of Cold War rivalry between the Soviet Union and the United States. It captured headlines in the late 1950s. On October 4, 1957, *Sputnik* (which means "fellow traveler" in Russian) was launched by the Soviet Union. The first satellite to investigate outer space, the aluminum sphere was about 22 inches (56 centimeters) in diameter. It weighed 184 pounds (83 kilograms). *Sputnik* carried a radio transmitter, and when it entered orbit, its bleeps were heard on radios around the world.

Americans were shocked and humiliated by this major Soviet accomplishment. People in the United States were ashamed that the Russians had moved ahead in developing new technology. Americans also knew that the accomplishment meant that Soviet missiles soon could carry nuclear warheads aimed at the United States.

The Soviets launched *Sputnik II* on November 3, 1957. On board was Laika, a dog that was the first living creature to travel in orbit. Laika did not survive the trip, but correcting the experiment's failures furthered the idea that humans could survive in the weightlessness of space.

U.S. scientists and military leaders demanded that the United States catch up with the Soviets. After many failed efforts, the United States finally succeeded. In Jan-

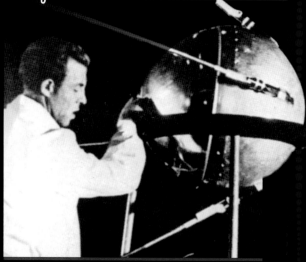

A Soviet scientist puts the finishing touches on *SPUTNIK* in 1957.

uary 1958, the rocket *Explorer* launched a satellite into orbit. Americans hailed *Explorer* with pride and relief. Soon additional U.S. satellites were orbiting Earth. The nation heard President Eisenhower's 1958 Christmas message relayed by satellite from outer space.

One of the lasting achievements of the space race was the National Defense Education Act of 1958. It required that taxpayers' money be provided to improve the country's educational system. The money included loans to college students majoring in engineering, science, and mathematics. The students went on to careers that helped propel the United States to lead the world in space exploration.

Scientists in the Soviet Union concentrated on developing missiles that could deliver nuclear bombs across long distances. In 1957 the Soviet Union tested the world's first intercontinental ballistic missile (ICBM). A short time later, the United States also developed the ICBM, and by the end of the 1950s, the U.S. missile program had surged ahead of the Soviets'.

■ "I LIKE IKE"

General Dwight D. "Ike" Eisenhower was a beloved American hero. He had led the Allied armies in Europe to victory in World War II before becoming commander of NATO forces. During the 1952 presidential campaign, Eisenhower ran as the Republican Party's nominee. Illinois governor Adlai Stevenson opposed him on the Democratic Party's ticket. Throughout the campaign, supporters of each candidate were easy to spot. Eisenhower's voters wore buttons proclaiming, "I Like Ike." Stevenson's supporters had their own slogan: "I'm Madly for Adlai."

On Election Day in November, Eisenhower won the presidency. He received 33,936,234 votes—more than any other presidential candidate in history up to that time. Stevenson won 27,314,992 votes. Eisenhower carried thirty-nine states with 442 electoral votes, while Stevenson won only nine states with 89 electoral votes.

■ EISENHOWER TRIES TO EASE TENSIONS

President Eisenhower was deeply concerned about the Cold War. In a speech to the UN in December 1953, he proposed the creation of an international agency that would safeguard the materials that are used to make nuclear weapons. His proposal led to the creation of the International Atomic Energy Agency (IAEA). But this organization did not stop the arms race between the United States and the Soviet Union, mostly because the Soviets perceived the IAEA as nothing more than U.S. propaganda.

A year and a half later, President Eisenhower attended a summit meeting at Geneva, Switzerland. At the summit (a conference of high-level officials), Eisenhower talked with Nikita Khrushchev, the head of the Soviet Union. The government leaders of Great Britain and France also attended.

31

PRESIDENT EISENHOWER *(second from right)*, **SOVIET LEADER NIKITA KHRUSHCHEV** *(left)*, and other leaders from the Soviet Union, Great Britain, France, and Switzerland attend a party following the Big Four Conference in Switzerland in 1955.

Eisenhower boldly called for a policy of openness. He asserted that the four countries should give one another blueprints of their military establishments and allow aerial inspections of these military bases. Historian Warren I. Cohen wrote, "Khrushchev, suspicious of American intentions, perhaps fearful that the United States would learn too much about [exactly how weak the Soviets were], was not interested." Khrushchev wanted Americans—and the rest of the world—to believe that the Soviets were a strong military power. While the Soviets did have a number of nuclear weapons, it took more than forty years for the world to learn the truth: the Soviets were not nearly as powerful as they had claimed.

Eisenhower's peace efforts were countered somewhat by Secretary of State John Foster Dulles. In January 1954, Dulles announced a policy that became known as massive retaliation. Dulles believed that the United States must be willing to go to the brink of war, if necessary, to protect U.S. interests. Critics of his policy called this policy "brinksmanship."

■ CRISIS IN SOUTHEAST ASIA

Events elsewhere in the world also challenged Eisenhower's foreign policy. After Japan surrendered Indochina (present-day Myanmar, Cambodia, Laos,

Malaysia, Thailand, and Vietnam) in 1945, the French attempted to resume pre-World War II occupation of their former colony. But the people of Indochina hated French rule and were eager to achieve independence. Their strongest leader was Ho Chi Minh, a Communist who had received military training in the Soviet Union and China. He headed a group called the Vietminh, which started a war in 1946 to drive the French out of Indochina.

The United States was unwilling to let Indochina fall to the Communists. President Eisenhower admitted that this region was of only slight importance to the United States. But he believed in "the 'domino theory': if Indochina fell [to Communists], the remaining states of Southeast Asia would fall [to Communist rule] one after another." To help prevent this, the United States sent about $1 billion a year in aid to the French in Indochina. Despite this financial help, in 1954 the French army in a key Vietnamese village called Dien Bien Phu was defeated following a two-month siege by the Communists.

After the fall of Dien Bien Phu, a multination conference divided the area of Indochina known as Vietnam into two parts, Communist North Vietnam and democratic South Vietnam. This temporary division was to be followed by an all-Vietnam election in 1956, but the election did not take place. Ho Chi Minh, who was confident he would win an election, did not care that it was delayed. He intended to use military force to bring about a united Communist Vietnam.

The United States sent financial aid and military advisers to South Vietnam, which was controlled by Ngo Dinh Diem. U.S. military forces did not become actively involved in the Vietnam War until 1964.

■ COMMUNISTS TAKE OVER HUNGARY

In 1956 the people of Hungary mounted the most serious challenge yet to Soviet rule in Eastern Europe. On November 1, Hungarian leader Imry Nagy protested Soviet troop movements in his country. He also rejected the Warsaw Pact, an agreement that bound the Soviet puppet states in a military alliance. Nagy then declared Hungary a democracy.

To put down this challenge, the Soviets sent thousands of troops and four thousand tanks to Budapest, Hungary's capital, on November 3. Many Hungarians believed that the United States would come to their aid. President Eisenhower, who was reelected as president three days after the Soviet troops moved into Budapest, issued a strong protest against the invasion. But he and his advisers decided that it was too dangerous to send military forces behind the iron curtain. They concluded that this would almost certainly trigger a nuclear war.

The UN tried to help. The General Assembly demanded that Soviet troops and tanks withdraw from Hungary, but Khrushchev refused. While the world looked on in horror, the Soviets ruthlessly overpowered the Hungarians. In Budapest alone, thousands of Hungarians were killed. Thousands more fled in panic for the nearby Austrian border (Austria was not controlled by the Soviets). The United States eventually allowed thirty thousand Hungarian refugees to enter the country.

■ THE EISENHOWER DOCTRINE

About the time of the Hungarian revolt, Egypt's president, Gamal Abdel Nasser, sent Egyptian troops to seize control of the Suez Canal. This important waterway in northeastern Egypt is a major transportation route for international trade. Nasser closed the waterway to shipping in July 1956, hurting U.S. and British trade. Previously, the canal had been open to all vessels except those from Israel, seen as the Arabs' chief enemy.

Fighting soon erupted when Israeli troops attacked Egypt and moved toward the canal. British and French troops then moved in and seized parts of the canal. Tensions rose further when the Soviet Union threatened to send troops to help defend Egypt. This action could have started a nuclear war against Britain and France.

The Soviet Union's position toward Egypt in the Suez Canal War appeared to open the door to establishing Communism in the oil-rich Middle East. To prevent this from happening, in January 1957, Congress gave President Eisenhower the power to use U.S. military forces to defend the Middle East. Known as the Eisenhower Doctrine, this policy told the world that the United States would not allow Communism to spread to the Middle East.

■ TROUBLE ON OUR DOORSTEP

On January 8, 1959, Fidel Castro led a band of Communist guerrillas (small fighting groups that rely on harassment and sabotage as their main weapons) in an overthrow of Fulgencio Batista, the dictator of Cuba. One month later, Castro named himself leader of that island country. He promised that he would bring sweeping changes to Cuba's government and economy, which many Cubans viewed as corrupt and repressive.

Many Cubans were hopeful at first. But then Castro's soldiers rounded up many of the people he considered to be his enemies. Some were publicly executed. Others were sentenced to long terms in prison. Many Cubans fled from their homeland when Castro seized power. About five hundred thousand Cuban exiles settled in or near Miami, Florida.

In May 1959, Castro, following the Communist principle of land redistribution, ordered many huge farms to be broken up. The land was then to be given to poor farmers. The Cuban government seized nearly 9 million acres (3.6 million hectares) of land, some belonging to U.S. companies. The following year, Castro demanded that oil refineries on the island, which were owned by Americans, refine oil that Cuba was receiving from the Soviet Union. When the oil companies refused, Castro seized the refineries.

The Eisenhower administration struck back. It put an embargo (prohibition) on all trade with Cuba. The embargo severely crippled the island's economy, which had depended on selling its huge sugar crop to the United States. That same year, however, Cuba made a major trade agreement with the Soviet Union, boosting Cuba's economy for a time.

Castro became a pro-Soviet Communist, and he formally announced his Communist beliefs in 1961. At about the same time that President Eisenhower was leaving office in January 1961, relations between the United States and Cuba were officially broken off. The presence of a Communist dictator in a place less than 100 miles (160 km) from the United States led to trouble on our doorstep in the years ahead.

FIDEL CASTRO speaks to reporters in April 1959. The Communist leader took power in Cuba in January 1959.

This 1957 Chevrolet Bel Air convertible has classic 1950s styling—TAIL FINS, CHROME TRIM, AND COMFORTABLE, ROOMY SEATS.

Chapter Three

BREAKTHROUGHS:

*Science, Technology, and
Transportation of the 1950s*

Life at home improved for Americans in the 1950s. Most families by then had vacuum cleaners and refrigerators. Smaller and lighter vacuum cleaners made it easier to remove dirt from carpets and rugs. Improved cooling technology in refrigerators made it possible to keep fresh and frozen foods longer than ever. The ever-growing assortment of frozen foods, first developed in the 1930s, reduced the number of trips Americans had to make to the grocery store. Some homes and most theaters and auditoriums had air-conditioning, which made life more comfortable during hot summers.

◼ LONGER LIVES

In the 1950s, people in the United States were living longer than ever before. With improvements in medicine and diet, they were generally about 3 inches (8 cm) taller than Americans at the beginning of the century. A woman in 1950 could expect to live to the age of seventy-one, twenty years longer than a woman in 1900. A man's life expectancy climbed from forty-eight to sixty-five. The overall population also was younger. Because of the post-World War II baby boom, which accounted for an incredible 40 million births from 1946 to 1964, about 40 percent of the people in the United States were under twenty years of age by the mid-1960s.

■ MAKING CHILDHOOD SAFE

Medical science made great progress in the 1950s. Penicillin, an antibiotic discovered in 1941, was used widely in the fifties. By the mid-1950s, scientists had introduced many other antibiotics to treat diseases such as pneumonia, tuberculosis, and rheumatic fever. Other medical accomplishments included organ transplants, advances in cancer research, the use of laser beams in surgery, and the production of synthetic (artificial) DNA (deoxyribonucleic acid, which carries genetic information in living things).

One of the decade's most remarkable medical achievements dramatically reduced the number of cases of poliomyelitis, or polio—a dreaded

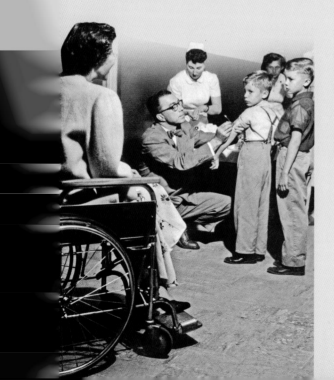

> ## " Risks, I like to say, always pay off. You learn what to do and what not to do. "

—Jonas Salk, discussing his work developing the polio vaccine, 1991

disease. In America in the 1950s, summer was a season of fear and anxiety for parents, because it was the season when children most commonly contracted polio. Many parents forbade their children from swimming in community pools or attending crowded events, where they believed their children would catch the crippling disease.

For many years, polio had killed or crippled more youngsters than any other communicable (transmittable) disease. After many years of painstaking research, Dr. Jonas Salk developed a polio vaccine in 1954. The following year, it was declared safe and effective. Only 910 polio cases were reported in 1962, an astounding decrease from 37,476 in 1954. The conquest of this disease was a victory of enormous importance, not only to people in the United States but throughout the world.

A mother who was stricken with polio in the early 1950s watches as her son receives **THE SALK POLIO VACCINE.**

Born in New York in 1914, Jonas Salk was one of four children. His parents encouraged him and his siblings to study hard and succeed in school. When Salk entered the City College of New York, he intended to study law but became fascinated by medicine instead.

While Salk attended medical school at New York University, he spent a year researching the virus that causes the flu. Salk wanted to find out if the virus itself could be used to give immunity (resistance) to people without infecting them. His success in this effort became the basis for his research on polio.

In 1947 Salk joined the University of Pittsburgh Medical School and devoted the next eight years to developing a polio vaccine. Salk's vaccine was made up of killed, or inactive, poliovirus. Because the virus was killed, it wouldn't make people sick. Salk believed people who were injected with it would develop antibodies and thus be protected from the disease. Salk tested the vaccine on himself, his wife, his children, and his staff. His test subjects developed anti-polio antibodies. "Risks, I like to say, always pay off," Salk said later. "You learn what to do and what not to do." National testing on Salk's vaccine began in 1954. The one million children, ages six to nine, who were injected with the vaccine were hailed as Polio Pioneers. The human

JONAS SALK conducts medical research in a lab in the 1950s.

testing proved the vaccine was safe and effective.

When news of Salk's discovery was made public on April 12, 1955, he became a hero to millions around the world. Salk refused to profit personally from the vaccine. He desired only that it be given to as many people as possible.

In 1963 Salk founded the Jonas Salk Institute for Biological Studies in California, where medical and scientific research is conducted. Salk spent the remainder of his career doing research, attempting to develop an AIDS vaccine, and writing books about medicine. He died on June 23, 1995.

FORTRAN, CORDLESS RADIOS, AND HI-FI

The 1950s was the decade that also produced some exciting new technologies. Computers came into much wider use, although they still were very large and unwieldy. For example, during the 1952 presidential election, the computers that tallied the votes occupied a space as large as the average American family's living room. Fortran, a programming language best suited to numeric and scientific computation, was developed by International Business Machines (IBM) in 1957.

There were also important developments in other electronics. For the first time, people had access to cordless transistor radios. They were battery-operated, and their small size made them portable. High fidelity, or hi-fi, which electronically reproduces sound without distortion, led to better-sounding recordings.

"SEE THE U.S.A. IN YOUR CHEVROLET"

The production and sale of automobiles in the United States increased phenomenally in the fifties. Beginning in 1950 and continuing for the rest of the decade, about 8 million cars were built every year. By 1958 about 68 million cars and trucks were in use, including more than one automobile for every household.

Manufacturers made cars that were larger, fancier, and faster than earlier models. Soaring tail fins, giant headlights, and shiny chrome became standard features. Popular cars included elegant Oldsmobiles and the new Packards, advertised as having the world's most powerful V-8 engines. But heading the list of cars intended for elite buyers were Cadillacs, which had the longest tail fins. A Cadillac ad said, "Fifty percent of all the motorists in America would rather own a Cadillac than any other automobile." The most expensive Cadillac was the Eldorado Brougham, which sold for about $14,000. (The average two-door car at that time was about $2,250.) It was fitted with a perfume bottle, a makeup case that included lipsticks, a tissue dispenser on the dashboard, and four gold-finished drinking cups.

Fast sports cars appealed to many people, especially the younger generation. The Chevrolet Corvette, which was introduced in 1953, became a favorite. The low, sleek, racy-looking Corvette coupe was likened by some enthusiasts to a flying saucer. Singer Dinah Shore appeared in TV commercials crooning the automaker's catchy jingle: "See the U.S.A. in your Chevrolet."

Beginning in the mid-1950s, some American customers began turning to smaller cars that cost less, got better gas mileage, and were easier to park. Germany's Volkswagen (VW) Beetle led in this field. VW sales in the United States were nearing two hundred thousand by 1957. Soon U.S. car manufacturers were also producing small compact cars.

The National Defense Highway Act of 1956 was a great boon to auto travelers. This act provided for the construction of 41,000 miles (66,000 km) of freeways and highways to be built over a ten-year period, at a cost of $26 billion. It was one of the largest public building projects in the history of the United States.

Driving swiftly along the new roadways without having to halt for numerous stoplights or slow down on bumpy gravel roads opened vast opportunities. In a relatively short travel time, Americans could visit faraway relatives and friends or travel to historic sites and national parks. The roadways spurred the growth of many industries that supported cars and road travel. These included oil, steel, and rubber industries; motels and hotels; gas stations; fast-food restaurants; and amusement centers such as Disneyland in Southern California, which opened in 1955. Interstates also fueled suburban development: Americans could live in the suburbs and commute easily to jobs in the cities.

The aviation industry saw major progress too. Previously Americans had relied on trains for long-distance travel in the United States and booked passage on ships to go overseas.

DISNEYLAND *(left)* opened in 1955. The nation's new highway system made vacations to amusement parks like Disneyland much easier.

In the United States, Pan American (Pan Am) Airlines inaugurated its transatlantic flights—from New York City to London, England—on October 26, 1958. The flight ushered in a new era in the history of passenger aviation. On that first flight, which made a stopover in Newfoundland, Canada, there were 111 passengers, the largest number ever to board a regularly scheduled flight up to that time. Coach fares were $272, or about $2,000 in early twenty-first century dollars.

Within the United States, National Airlines was the first to begin jet service, on December 10, 1958. American Airlines offered the first domestic jet service using its own aircraft on January 25, 1959, with a flight from New York City to Los Angeles, California. By the early 1960s, jets were flying routes all over the world.

Like modern planes, early planes included seat belts and safety presentations. The safety presentations were conducted by flight attendants who, because they were almost always female, were called stewardesses, or hostesses. The seats were much larger and more comfortable than those in present-day planes. Meals and beverages were served on every flight, and free gum was offered to each passenger. Smoking was allowed on planes. Many planes also had lounges where passengers could relax, dine, and socialize. For passengers, flights meant more comfort, less noise, and shorter travel times than on ocean liners, which had previously been the best mode of travel to overseas destinations. The revolution in technology that made jet travel possible made the world an even smaller place.

AIRLINE PASSENGERS EAT A MEAL during their flight in the late 1950s.

Jet planes had previously been used only by the armed forces, but the first U.S. commercial jet airliner flew on December 10, 1958. Its first flight was from New York City to Miami, Florida. Soon other jet planes were flying to many parts of the nation and across oceans to foreign destinations.

■ A MAJOR NEW WATER ROUTE

With no direct access to oceans, the Midwest of the United States was handicapped in trade with Europe and other continents. But this problem was solved in the 1950s by the construction of the Saint Lawrence Seaway.

The seaway was jointly constructed by the United States and Canada. Work on it began in 1954, and it opened for travel in 1959. The new seaway extended from the Gulf of Saint Lawrence in eastern Canada through the Great Lakes to the western end of Lake Superior. It enabled ships to journey 2,300 miles (3,700 km) from the Atlantic Ocean into the center of the American continent. A series of fifteen locks (enclosures to raise or lower vessels as they pass from one level of water to another) lifted ships about 600 feet (183 m) above sea level by the time they reached Lake Superior.

The waterway linked more than fifty port cities to faraway destinations. Cities on the shores of the Great Lakes that produced metal ore and manufactured goods, as well as processing farm products from surrounding areas, were able to trade with larger markets. Global trade improved midwestern economies and expanded the American economic landscape as never before.

43

A ship travels through a lock on the newly opened **SAINT LAWRENCE SEAWAY** in 1959.

A shopper pays for his purchase with an AMERICAN EXPRESS CREDIT CARD.
The advent of the credit card would shape the American economy for years to come.

Chapter Four

GOOD TIMES:
The 1950s Economy

Except for brief recessions (economic downturns) in 1953 and 1957
1958, large numbers of Americans enjoyed prosperity in the 1950s.
"Even the American taste for [excess] was stretched by the nature of the
good times in the fifties," observed historian Harold Evans. "There had
been nothing like it before in the history of the world."

Personal incomes more than doubled between 1950 and 1960, from
$2,992 in 1950 to about $6,000 in 1960. The number of people who held
jobs rose from about 53 million in 1950 to more than 70 million by 1960.

Stock market prices soared to a new high. Basic industries such as
automobiles, steel, and oil flourished.

■ "CHARGE IT!"

Though credit had been an important concept for much of human history,
people historically used cash to pay for purchases. Layaway was also a
means to buy an item without paying the entire cost at once. Rather than
take the item home and pay for it over time, people made payments at
the store and took the item home when it was fully paid for.

Born in Chicago, Illinois, Ray Kroc (1902–1984) was a traveling salesman. He became the exclusive distributor of a milk shake mixer called the Multimixer. Any restaurant that wanted the Multimixer had to buy it from Kroc. The Multimixer was an innovation because it could mix five milk shakes at once.

THE FIRST MCDONALD'S DRIVE-IN was built in 1955 in Des Plaines, Illinois.

In 1954 Kroc heard about a hamburger stand in San Bernardino, California, called McDonald's. There, eight Multimixers ran at a time, nearly all day long, which meant the stand was popular among customers. Kroc drove from Illinois to California to see the business for himself.

When Kroc pulled in to the stand, he was amazed to see many customers being served very quickly. Richard and Maurice McDonald, the brothers who owned the stand, explained that with only hamburgers, french fries, and milk shakes on the menu, ordering, cooking, and serving customers could be done rapidly. This made it possible for many customers to be served more quickly than in usual sit-down restaurants with multiple offerings on the menu. Kroc suggested the McDonalds open several restaurants. The three became business partners.

The first McDonald's drive-in restaurant—with the now familiar golden arches—opened in Des Plaines, Illinois, in 1955. Hamburgers cost 15 cents apiece and fries 10 cents per serving. Milk shakes made in the Multimixer sold for 20 cents.

Kroc went on to build the restaurant chain on the concepts of a limited menu, strict quality control, and massive advertising. By 1961 there were more than 130 McDonald's restaurants in the United States. In that same year, Kroc bought the company from the McDonald brothers for $2.7 million. Kroc went on to build an empire, which, by the time he died in 1984, had 8,300 restaurants in thirty-four countries with annual sales of more than $10 billion.

In the 2000s, McDonald's is the largest fast-food restaurant chain in the world, serving 47 million customers a day. There are more than 30,000 restaurants in one hundred countries, and annual sales of more than $23 billion. No longer a restaurant, the first McDonald's is now a museum containing McDonald's memorabilia and artifacts—including Kroc's Multimixer, which started it all.

By the mid-1900s, many stores and gas stations were offering their own credit cards. Customers paid their balances monthly. This convenience, however, resulted in some customers having dozens of credit cards. In 1950 a credit card that could be used at more than one merchant was invented when Frank X. McNamara and two friends started the Diners Club. Instead of individual companies offering credit to their own customers, whom they would bill later, ways for creditors to make money were introduced much later.)

The first Diners Club cards were given out in 1950 to two hundred people and were accepted by fourteen restaurants in New York. The cards were made of thick paper, not plastic, and the restaurants that accepted it were printed on the back. The concept of the credit card grew quickly, and by the end of 1950, twenty thousand people were using the Diners Club card. The Diners

> " Even the American taste for [excess] was stretched by the nature of the good times in the fifties. There had been nothing like it before in the history of the world."

—*historian Harold Evans,* The American Century, *1998*

the Diners Club offered credit to customers on behalf of many companies. Then Diners Club billed the customers and paid the companies. The Diners Club wasn't selling anything itself, so to make money, it charged companies who accepted the card 7 percent of the amount of each transaction. Subscribers paid a $3 annual fee. (Interest-bearing credit cards as

Club grew in popularity and had no competition until 1958. In that year, both American Express and the BankAmericard (later called Visa) came into use. Thousands of businesses began to accept credit cards, making it easier for customers to "charge it," and the concept of a universal credit card spread quickly around the world.

47

	1950s	2000s (first decade)
Average U.S. worker's income	$2,992	$35,000

TYPICAL PRICES

	1950s	2000s
Postage stamp	3¢	42¢
Loaf of bread	7¢	$2.79
Candy bar	10¢	75¢
Bottle of soda	15¢	$1.00
Quart of milk	21¢	$1.79
Gallon of gas	23¢	$2.80
Movie ticket	50¢	$9.00
Eggs (per dozen)	72¢	$2.99
Man's haircut	$1.00	$30.00
Denim jeans	$3.00	$25.00
Washing machine	$200.00	$809.00
Two-door car	$2,250	$20,000
Three-bedroom house	$12,000	$300,000

(Prices are samples only. At any given time, prices vary by year, location, size, brand, and model.)

48

AMERICA IN THE 1950s

■ AND TWO MORE MAKE FIFTY

Two more states—Alaska and Hawaii—were added to the United States in 1959. Russia had sold Alaska to the United States in 1867. Few Americans at the time could imagine what possible use or interest the 586,000 square miles (1.5 million sq. km) of land would have for the United States. However, when gold was first discovered there (in the 1870s) and then vast reserves of oil (in 1901), it became clear that Alaska had much to contribute to the U.S. economy. After Alaska became the forty-ninth state on January 3, 1959, the new U.S. flag featured seven rows of seven stars each.

The U.S. flag was revised again just seven months later when Hawaii became

HAWAII HAD A HUGE BOOST IN TOURISM DURING THE 1950s, which led, in part, to its becoming the fiftieth state in 1959.

the union's fiftieth state. Hawaii had been a U.S. territory since 1900. It became an important staging area for U.S. forces in the Pacific during World War II. The 1950s saw Hawaii develop major tourist and manufacturing industries. After it became a state on August 21, 1959, the flag was changed to its current design: nine horizontal rows of six stars (at the top and bottom) alternating with rows of five stars.

In general, American women and men fell into stereotypical roles during much of the 1950s—WOMEN STAYED HOME AND CARED FOR THE CHILDREN, while men earned money outside of the home.

Chapter Five

REVOLUTIONARY CHANGES:
Society in the 1950s

D uring World War II, many American men were serving in the armed forces. So millions of U.S. women, including those who were married, worked in defense plants or industries. After the men returned home from the war, this situation changed dramatically. With a prospering U.S. economy in which men alone generally could support their families, women left the workforce in huge numbers.

The decade saw the continuation of the social formula in which many young women got married shortly after finishing high school. Many Americans believed that the only reason for a young woman to attend college was to find a suitable husband. As a result, most high schools and colleges required girls and young women to attend home economics, or "home ec," classes. These classes taught the basics of cooking, baking, laundry, house cleaning, and sewing—everything young women needed to know to be skilled housewives. The focus on being prepared for marriage led to home ec classes being called "Mrs. degrees."

The lives of married women in the fifties generally revolved around taking care of their homes and families. Women's intelligence, energy, and creativity were funneled into home and family life. Some Americans began to wonder whether women who had come to enjoy their independence in the 1940s actually wanted to give up working outside the home. The professions, except for teaching and nursing, were virtually closed to married women. Most of the jobs available to them paid poorly. Some people began to wonder if this was fair.

SENATOR MARGARET CHASE SMITH was one of the first to publicly criticize Joseph McCarthy's hunt for Communists in the U.S. government.

In spite of these stirrings, women's rights made no significant gains in the 1950s. However, a minority that at first quietly wondered if there was more to life than cooking and cleaning would grow to have their voices heard in the next decade. Along with gains in employment, the opportunity for large numbers of women to be elected to local, state, and national government positions would occur later. All the same, there were women in American government in the 1950s. Senator Margaret Chase Smith from Maine, for example, made a splash in June 1950, when she criticized Senator Joseph McCarthy for his political attacks on alleged U.S. Communists. After her speech, she got the nickname Moscow Maggie, in reference to the capital of the Soviet Union.

◼ THE BABY BOOM CONTINUES

The massive increase in births that began after World War II is called the baby boom. Beginning in 1946, it continued through the fifties, ending in 1964. During those years, more than 76 million babies were born in the United States. The postwar good times were reflected in parents' attitudes toward children. Parents who had grown up during the Great Depression (1929–1942) were a generation well acquainted with poverty. Millions had grown up without the security of a home or a parent with a job. By the 1950s, as adults with jobs in a prosperous economy, they were able to indulge their children in ways they themselves had not experienced. They responded enthusiastically to one of the best-selling books of the decade, *The Common Sense Book of Baby and Child Care*. Written by Dr. Benjamin Spock and first published in 1946, the book gained popularity in the 1950s because it contradicted long-held beliefs about baby and child care. For example, standard practice was to feed babies according to a regular schedule, whether or not the babies were hungry. Spock recommended a more relaxed approach to feedings. He also advised parents to hug and kiss their children, uncommon advice for the era.

Benjamin Spock was born on May 2, 1903, in New Haven, Connecticut. He was the oldest of six children. Educated at Yale University in New Haven, Spock was on the crew team that won a gold medal at the 1924 Olympics. After spending the summer as a counselor at a camp for crippled children, he decided on a career in medicine. Following graduation from Yale, he attended medical school at Columbia University in New York. Spock worked as a pediatrician (a doctor who treats children) from 1933 to 1943. He also taught at New York's Cornell University medical school. At night, he worked on the book that would become *The Common Sense Book of Baby and Child Care.*

Dr. Spock had served as a psychiatrist in the U.S. Naval Reserve for two years during World War II. His book was first published in 1946. An instant best seller, the guide gained in reputation and importance as parents flocked to buy copies. Spock spent the 1950s teaching child develop-

DR. SPOCK gave parenting advice to millions through columns, books, and speeches in the 1950s.

ment and began writing a column that appeared regularly in women's magazines, first in *Ladies Home Journal* and later in *Redbook*. He became a political activist in the 1960s and updated *Baby and Child Care* several times before his death in 1998 at the age of ninety-four.

53

■ MOVING TO THE SUBURBS

During the Great Depression of the 1930s and World War II of the 1940s, the United States saw limited construction of new houses. But in the prosperous fifties, with the U.S. population soaring, this situation changed dramatically. Americans had more money to spend on new homes.

The federal government helped people achieve their goal of owning a new home. The Federal Housing

Administration (FHA) and the Veterans Administration (VA), which served the needs of former military personnel, were established in the 1930s. These government agencies made it possible for millions of people to buy single-family houses with low down payments and inexpensive, long-term loans.

In 1950 alone, 1.4 million new housing units were constructed. A large number of these homes were not built in existing cities but in suburbs. American families wanted to live where there was less traffic and noise; cleaner air; reduced crime; more green lawns, trees, and flower beds; and better schools for their children. Racial factors, too, contributed to the move out of cities. As urban neighborhoods and schools became increasingly populated by minorities, especially African Americans, white Americans moved to the suburbs. The idea of living in racially mixed neighborhoods was not commonly accepted at this time, when integration was a radical, new idea. This exodus of white families to suburbs was known as white flight. "The 1960 census revealed that while central cities had grown about 25 percent in population since 1950, the suburbs

had increased over 50 percent. Several central cities, including Detroit, Michigan; St. Louis, Missouri; San Francisco, California; and Washington, D.C., actually lost population, something unprecedented in the history of American cities."

In 1950 alone, 1.4 million new housing units were constructed. A large number of these homes were not built in existing cities but in suburbs.

To service the sprouting American suburbs, shopping centers were quickly erected. They were filled with stores, offices, and gas stations. This enabled suburbanites to travel only short distances to purchase the products they needed. They could also sneak in a visit to the offices of doctors, dentists, and lawyers there.

■ LEVITTOWN

Many builders of new suburban homes popped up, but the most famous was William Levitt, whose picture appeared on the cover of *Time* magazine on July 3, 1950. When Levitt opened his first sales office for homes he had built in Nassau County, outside New York City, on March 7, 1949, more than one thousand customers were waiting. They wanted to be among the first to buy the basic four-room houses for sixty-nine hundred dollars. Levittown, as the development was known, was very successful. Eventually it had thousands of homes that were occupied by more than eighty-two thousand people.

William Levitt borrowed Henry Ford's mass-production system used at the large Ford automobile plant in Detroit, Michigan. But instead of producing cars on an assembly line, Levitt had a different kind of assembly line. It consisted of mobile teams of workers, each doing a specific job on a specific site, until the houses were complete. It was, Levitt noted, like clockwork. "Eighteen houses completed on the shift from 8 to noon, and 18 more houses finished on the shift from 12:30 to 4:30."

Levitt construction crews first flattened a plot of land with a bulldozer and then laid concrete slabs for a home's foundation. This meant that the houses had no basements. Street

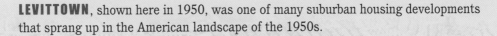

LEVITTOWN, shown here in 1950, was one of many suburban housing developments that sprang up in the American landscape of the 1950s.

pavers followed, then electricians with light poles, and then workers putting up street signs.

Teams of Levitt's workers then constructed the houses' frames. Still another team nailed down the floors. Crews moved in to install siding.

clotheslines on Mondays, but never on Sundays. Fences were forbidden. Lawns had to be cut regularly.

Even if families didn't want their houses to look like everyone else's, they were restricted to decorating only the inside differently. Also, since

According to Levitt's orders, nearly everything was uniform. . . . To those who previously had lived in crowded city apartments or postwar cramped government housing, their new houses were no less enjoyable because they had been built according to William Levitt's exact specifications.

Other crews installed flooring, sinks, bathtubs, and toilets. Workers used spray guns to paint the exterior and interior of each house. Spray guns made it possible to apply paint faster than workers using paintbrushes or rollers. Levitt built eight community swimming pools for the people of Levittown to enjoy. Land was set aside for schools, houses of worship, and playgrounds.

According to Levitt's orders, nearly everything was uniform. Trees were planted exactly 28 feet (8.5 meters) apart. Levitt decreed that laundry could be hung out to dry on backyard

doorbells and buzzers were prohibited, Levittown homeowners had to use chimes. However, residents were allowed to vary the pitch of their chimes, to distinguish them from other homeowners' chimes. To those who previously had lived in crowded city apartments or postwar cramped government housing, their new houses were no less enjoyable because they had been built according to William Levitt's exact specifications.

After the first Levittown was completed, William Levitt acquired 8 square miles (21 sq. km) on the Delaware River in Pennsylvania. For

Levittown II, there were eleven hundred streets that had not only houses, schools, places of worship, and swimming pools but also a shopping center, a railroad station, and baseball diamonds. Soon it had the tenth-largest population of any place in Pennsylvania. Levitt proudly called it "the most perfectly planned community in America."

Builders throughout the country followed Levitt's lead, and new suburbs sprang up in many states. For example, in Lakewood, California, as many as 100 houses were started each day. In less than three years, 17,500 houses were erected. "By 1955, *House and Garden* magazine reported that suburbia had become 'the national way of life.'"

Many Americans, however—especially black Americans—did not have the opportunity to experience life in the new suburbs. Some people were too poor to move out of the cities, or they had to remain there to work. Large numbers of urban dwellers continued to live in crowded cities, and many farmers stayed where they tilled the land.

While many Americans enjoyed new opportunities in the suburbs, others continued to live in crowded cities such as **BROOKLYN, NEW YORK**.

AFRICAN AMERICANS SEEK RACIAL JUSTICE

At the beginning of the 1950s, discrimination against African Americans was part of everyday life. In some parts of the United States, blacks were barred from hotels and restaurants that served white patrons. Segregation was especially prevalent throughout the South. There, laws required blacks to attend separate places of worship and segregated schools that were usually inferior to the schools for white students. African Americans had to sit in specified sections of buses, trains, theaters, and ballparks. They had to use separate restrooms and water fountains. Blacks lived in certain parts of southern towns and cities, where the housing was generally inadequate and drinking unclean water led to a variety of diseases. Black patients usually were treated only by black doctors, and were denied admission to most whites-only clinics and hospitals.

Lynchings (murders, such as hangings, at the hands of white mobs) and other physical abuses of African Americans occurred in many places throughout the South. Destructive raids by white supremacist groups such as the Ku Klux Klan (KKK) struck terror in the hearts of their targets, who included African Americans, Catholics, and other groups.

Denied the right to vote throughout nearly all the South, blacks appeared to have little chance to escape these conditions. This was largely because U.S. law allowed for "separate but equal" facilities, such as schools and restrooms, for African Americans. These places were almost never equal, however, because white southerners regarded blacks as inferior.

A 1954 COURT DECISION AGAINST SEGREGATION

Five legal attacks on school segregation reached the U.S. Supreme Court in 1952, with cases filed in Kansas, Virginia, South Carolina, Delaware, and the District of Columbia. The justices placed all five cases under a single name, *Brown v. Board of Education of Topeka, Kansas.*

Brown v. Board of Education stemmed from an African American man in Kansas named Oliver Brown who had sued Topeka's board of education on behalf of his daughter Linda. She had been forced to travel a long distance to a run-down school for blacks. Linda had to walk six blocks through a dangerous railroad yard and then take a bus for another twenty-one blocks.

EMMETT TILL posed for this photograph with his mother, Mamie Bradley, in the early 1950s. Till's murder in 1955 and the subsequent acquittal of his killers helped spark the civil rights movement.

In the wake of the Supreme Court ruling in *Brown v. Board of Education*, violence against African Americans occurred in various parts of the country. In August 1955, Emmett Till, a black fourteen-year-old from Chicago, Illinois, was visiting his great-uncle, Moses Wright, in Mississippi. Exact details are unclear, but Till is said to have spoken inappropriately to a white woman. As a result, two white men, including the woman's husband, kidnapped Till from Wright's home during the night. One of them shot the boy in the head. Then they wired his body to a heavy piece of metal and threw it in a river. Witnesses identified the murderers to federal agents, but an all-white, twelve-man jury acquitted the men. (Blacks and white women were barred from serving as jurors in Mississippi at that time.)

Five days after the murder, Till's body was returned to Chicago for a funeral. The boy's mother, Mamie, insisted that the casket be left open so that the world could see "what [the killers] did to my boy." Emmett's face was battered beyond recognition and he had a bullet hole in his head. The body was badly decomposed after spending a few days underwater. During the next four days, thousands of people filed past the casket. Photographs of Till's body were published in magazines and newspapers, shocking and outraging Americans—black and white—from coast to coast. The story became international news.

Shortly after their acquittal, Till's murderers confessed to a reporter that they had been responsible for his death. The case was not retried, because U.S. law prevents anyone from being tried twice for the same crime.

One hundred days after Till's murder, Rosa Parks refused to give up her seat on the city bus in Montgomery, Alabama, beginning the city's bus boycott. While Parks is often credited with sparking the civil rights movement, many modern historians contend that the movement truly began with Till's murder.

A whites-only school with better facilities and more experienced teachers was only seven blocks from her home. Oliver Brown believed that his daughter should be permitted to attend this more conveniently located school that offered better educational opportunities.

The National Association for the Advancement of Colored People (NAACP) hired Thurgood Marshall, an African American attorney, to represent Brown. Marshall argued before the U.S. Supreme Court that segregation made equal education impossible and that separate schools damaged black youngsters by making them feel inferior.

The Supreme Court's May 17, 1954, decision was unanimous—and history making. The justices concluded that segregation was illegal. Writing for the Court, Chief Justice Earl Warren said, "We conclude that in the field of public education the doctrine of 'separate but equal' has no place. Separate educational facilities are inherently unequal." African Americans were jubilant. They knew this meant the beginning of the end of legal segregation in the United States.

The Supreme Court did not offer specifics on how the states should change their school systems to eliminate segregation. Gradually, some states worked toward reducing segregation. After many months, Texas, West Virginia, Tennessee, Maryland, Arkansas, and Delaware reported partial integration in their schools.

THURGOOD MARSHALL *(center)* along with George E. C. Hayes *(left)* and James M. Nabrit *(right)* won their case against school segregation on May 17, 1954. The three pose together in front of the Supreme Court after the victory.

However, state and community leaders in the Deep South reacted differently. The Deep South is made up of Alabama, Georgia, Louisiana, Mississippi, North Carolina, and South Carolina. Parts of Florida, Virginia, Tennessee, Arkansas, and Texas are also considered part of the Deep South. There, reaction to *Brown v. Board of Education* was hostile. Some states, including South Carolina and Georgia, threatened to close their public schools rather than integrate them.

"We conclude that in the field of public education the doctrine of 'separate but equal' has no place. Separate educational facilities are inherently unequal."

—*Chief Justice Earl Warren, in the Supreme Court's* **Brown v. Board of Education** *ruling, 1954*

■ THE CRISIS AT LITTLE ROCK

The most difficult battle for school integration erupted in Little Rock, Arkansas. Shortly after the *Brown v. Board of Education* decision, the Little Rock school board approved a plan for gradual desegregation starting at the high school level. Arkansas's medical and law schools already had been integrated. Nine black students were scheduled to join the two thousand white students when Central High School opened for the new school year on September 3, 1957.

By the time the first class bell sounded at Central High School, an angry white mob had gathered in front of the school to prevent the black students from entering. Frightened, the students went home. Governor Orval Faubus—who had said that "blood will run in the streets" before African American students would be allowed into Central High—called on the state's National Guard to block the students from entering the school. President Eisenhower met with Faubus and tried to get him to send the Guard troops home. The governor refused.

On September 24, President Eisenhower took action. He sent in troops to take over the National Guard and protect the nine black students when they entered the high school. These soldiers guarded the students for months, until tempers eased, safety was ensured, and calm was restored.

Known in modern history books as the Little Rock Nine, the nine black students who integrated Central High School are regarded as heroes of the civil rights movement. The nine are Ernest Green, Elizabeth Eckford, Jefferson Thomas, Dr. Terrence Roberts, Carlotta Walls Lanier, Minnijean Brown Trickey, Gloria Ray Karlmark, Thelma Mothershed-Wair, and Melba Pattillo Beals. All credit their parents as the real heroes, because it was their parents who convinced them that they deserved the same educational op-portunities as white students. A year after integrating the school, Green was its first black graduate.

Central High School became Central High School National Historic Site in 1998. It is preserved as a symbol of the struggle over school desegregation. The Little Rock Nine were awarded the Congressional Gold Medal—one of the nation's highest civilian honors—in 1999. Also in 1999, the nine established the Little Rock Nine Foundation. It works to bring better educational opportunities to young people in poor schools.

Soldiers escorted the LITTLE ROCK NINE into Little Rock Central High School on September 25, 1957.

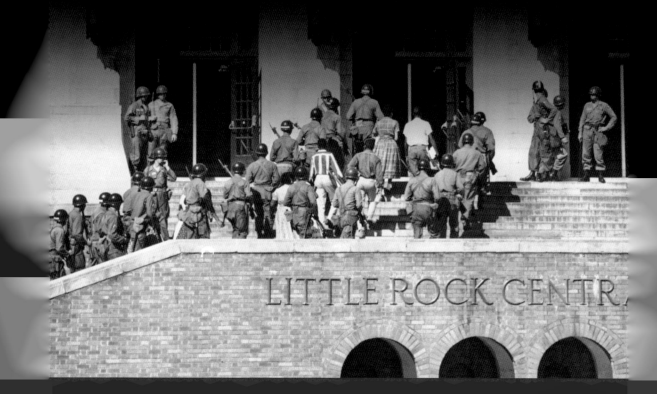

The crisis at Little Rock was the first time since the period following the U.S. Civil War (1861–1865) that federal troops had been sent to the South to preserve order. It seemed that *Brown v. Board of Education*, which had held the promise of equality for all students, was only a partial victory in the long struggle to achieve civil rights for all Americans.

■ THE MONTGOMERY BUS BOYCOTT

Rosa Parks had endured the unfairness of the city bus service in Montgomery, Alabama, all of her life. She and other African Americans had to sit in the back of city buses. When the white sections were filled, blacks had to stand so white people could sit in their seats.

On December 1, 1955, Parks—a secretary for the Montgomery chapter of the NAACP—challenged Alabama's segregation law. When a white man boarded the crowded city bus she was riding, the bus driver ordered her to give up her seat. Refusing to do so, she was arrested and jailed.

The Reverend E. D. Nixon, the head of the NAACP in Montgomery, bailed Parks out of jail and asked her to be the central figure in a case challenging segregation before a federal court. She agreed.

The following Monday, Nixon also decided that all the city's African Americans should boycott Montgomery's bus system. He enlisted about fifty black ministers, who passed the message to their congregations at Sunday church services. Among them was the new twenty-six-year-old preacher at the Dexter Avenue Baptist Church, Martin Luther King Jr.

On Monday morning, the buses had no African American passengers, even though blacks usually made up the largest group of bus riders. Later that day, King addressed the bus boycott at his church. Every seat was taken, and many in the crowd—estimated at between ten thousand and fifteen thousand—had to listen from speakers installed outside the building.

ROSA PARKS sits in the front of a bus in Montgomery, Alabama, after the successful bus boycott of 1956.

King declared that the time had come for oppression against African Americans to end. He encouraged black Americans to use nonviolent means to secure their rights.

This was the beginning of King's career as the nation's foremost leader in the struggle to achieve civil rights for African Americans. The key to King's enormous success was his absolute insistence that the movement he championed be carried out in a nonviolent, peaceful manner. King was inspired by the examples of Jesus Christ, who preached love for one's enemies, and by Mohandas Gandhi, the leader of India's movement to end British rule in that country in the 1930s and 1940s. Like them, King told his followers to meet hate with love.

The black community in Montgomery responded wholeheartedly to the bus boycott. More than three hundred volunteers drove the boycotters in cars and cabs from their homes to their work sites and back again. Other African Americans traveled long distances on foot or by bicycle.

Nearly one year later, on November 13, 1956, the U.S. Supreme Court declared, in an unrelated case, that all laws

THE REVEREND MARTIN LUTHER KING JR.
speaks to an overflow crowd at Holt Street Baptist Church in Mongomery, Alabama, in 1955. The huge crowd met to plan the Montgomery bus boycott.

requiring bus segregation were unconstitutional. The Montgomery Bus Boycott immediately ended. King then boarded a city bus and sat in a front seat. Afterward, he said that it was a great ride.

■ THE GOVERNMENT ACKNOWLEDGES GOD

Americans—both at home and those serving overseas—turned to religion for comfort and strength during the World War II years. With a new conflict in Korea and the tensions of the Cold War, many Americans continued to turn to religion in the 1950s. Families attended weekly religious services, and the Sabbath (days set aside for worship and rest) was generally reserved for visiting relatives.

One of the first references to the national motto, "In God We Trust," was included in "The Star-Spangled Banner." Written as a poem in 1814 by Francis Scott Key, it was later set to music and became the U.S. national anthem. The motto was first placed on coins in 1864, during the Civil War. By 1909 it was included on most coins. On July 11, 1955, during the height of the Cold War, President Eisenhower signed a law that required the motto to be displayed on all U.S. coinage and paper currency. It was meant as a way to show the United States' superiority over Communist countries, particularly the Soviet Union, where freedom of religion did not exist.

The Pledge of Allegiance is the oath of loyalty to the flag of the United States and to the nation it symbolizes. Many schoolchildren recite the pledge at the beginning of each school day, and public officials, such as city council and school board members, often recite it. The houses of the U.S. Congress open their daily sessions by reciting the pledge. Until 1954 the pledge did not include the words "under God."

President Abraham Lincoln had described the United States as a nation "under God" in his Gettysburg Address of 1863. Beginning in 1952, religious organizations and well-known ministers began to note that the pledge, as written, could apply to any country. They believed that by including the words "under God," the United States would distinguish itself as the moral country Lincoln described. President Eisenhower agreed. On June 14, 1954, he signed a law that required the words be added to the pledge.

Deborah Kerr and Burt Lancaster appear in a steamy scene from the 1953 movie *FROM HERE TO ETERNITY* based on James Jones's 1951 book of the same name.

Chapter Six

VOICES:
Writing of the 1950s

With the arrival of television in the American living room, many people thought the sale of books would decline dramatically. They were soon proven wrong. In the 1950s, 53 percent more books were sold than in the 1940s.

Military themes were highlighted in some of the best sellers, partly because readers linked them to their ongoing concerns about the Cold War. *From Here to Eternity* (1951), by James Jones, tells about army life in Hawaii. Herman Wouk's Pulitzer Prize-winning novel, *The Caine Mutiny* (1951), depicts the rebellion of a disgruntled naval crew against their captain.

J. D. Salinger's *The Catcher in the Rye* was published in 1951. Its chief characters are teens who feel trapped in a conformist world in which people strive to act only according to established standards or customs. The book had a strong appeal among teenage readers. Salinger followed *Catcher* with a short-story collection, *Nine Stories* (1953).

Ernest Hemingway's *The Old Man and the Sea* (1952) won the Pulitzer Prize. In 1954 Hemingway was awarded the Nobel Prize in Literature for the short novel.

In 1958 Boris Pasternak's *Doctor Zhivago* was a fascinating account of the 1917 Communist revolution in Russia. The novel was later made into a successful movie starring Julie Christie and Omar Sharif as the star-crossed lovers. The following year, Leon Uris's *Exodus* dealt with the important story of the birth of Israel after World War II. In a single year, *Doctor Zhivago* sold five hundred thousand copies and *Exodus* sold four hundred thousand copies. John Knowles's coming-of-age novel, *A Separate Peace*, debuted in 1959. Readers related to its timeless themes of identity, loss of childhood innocence, resentment, and envy.

J. D. Salinger was born in New York City on January 1, 1919. He attended high school at a private school in Pennsylvania, where he began writing stories. He enrolled in New York University but dropped out after a short time. In 1941 Salinger began submitting stories to a variety of magazines for publication. After a series of rejections, one of his works was published in the *New Yorker*, a widely circulated magazine. When the United States entered World War II in December 1941, Salinger was drafted into the army.

After the war ended in 1945, he returned to his work as a writer. By 1950 he had turned Holden Caulfield, a character from one of his rejected works, into the main character in *The Catcher in the Rye*. Salinger's first novel, it was published in 1951 to mixed reviews. Some critics called it "an unusually brilliant first novel." Others rejected it because of Holden's use of religious slurs and casual discussions of sex and prostitution. Within two months of its publication, the novel was listed on the *New York Times* best-seller list, where it remained for thirty weeks. The novel is considered one of the defining works of the decade for adolescents, becoming "the book all brooding adolescents had to buy." Newspapers began publishing articles about the "Catcher Cult," and the novel was banned in several countries—as well

This photograph of **J. D. SALINGER** was taken in 1951, the same year his most famous novel, *The Catcher in the Rye*, was published.

as some U.S. schools—which only contributed to its popularity.

Salinger was uncomfortable with the attention that resulted from his fame and became increasingly reclusive. Though he continued writing short stories, he never again published another novel. His last published work appeared in 1965. His last interview occurred in 1980. Salinger lives in Cornish, New Hampshire, with his wife but is seldom seen in public.

Truman Capote wrote short stories, novels, plays, and nonfiction works, many of which are among the most recognized works of American literature. His writing career spanned five decades, but one of his most popular works, the short novel *Breakfast at Tiffany's*, was published in 1958. Capote's novel, *The Grass Harp* (1951) was also made into a play. It explores the relationship between an orphan boy and two elderly women who are misfits in their society. The novel paralleled U.S. society of the time, in which conformity was common and nonconformists felt shunned.

Two African American authors, James Baldwin and Ralph Ellison, wrote their most important works during the fifties. Baldwin wrote novels, essays, plays, and poems, many of which examined racial issues in the United States as well as tackling the then-taboo subject of homosexuality. Baldwin's first novel, *Go Tell It on the Mountain* (1953) is a largely autobiographical account of the Christian church in the lives of African Americans. It examines how the church was both a source of inspiration as well as moral hypocrisy in the segregated United States. Ellison's best-known work, *Invisible Man*, won the National Book Award in 1953. The novel explores the search of an unnamed black man in New York City for his identity and place in society. Ellison's work was unique among authors of the time because he created characters who were educated and articulate. These characters challenged many Americans' stereotypical views of African Americans as poorly educated and unintelligent.

■ THE BEATS STIR A MOVEMENT

Two writers, Jack Kerouac and Allen Ginsberg, became early literary leaders of the so-called Beat Generation. The Beat Generation rejected society's conventional standards and strove for artistic self-expression. In his 1957 best seller, *On the Road*, Kerouac struck out fiercely against the established culture and lifestyles of the United States. Poet Ginsberg did the same in his long poem *Howl*, which he first read in public in 1955.

A third Beat Generation writer, William S. Burroughs, was a novelist, essayist, painter, and social critic. His novel *Naked Lunch* was first published in the United States in 1958. Burroughs's works were influenced by his homosexuality and drug addiction, uncommon literary themes at the time. His

Beat Generation writers **JACK KEROUAC** *(second from left, facing camera)* and **ALLEN GINSBERG** *(right)* are joined by fellow artists Larry Rivers *(left)*, Gregory Corso *(back of head)*, and David Amram *(second from right)* at a restaurant in New York in the late 1950s.

works are populated by nonconformists and antisocial characters. The beats (or beatniks) of the 1950s influenced many of the leaders of social movements of the next decade.

■ WOMEN WRITERS MAKE THEIR MARK

During the 1950s, women writers struggled to be heard. Often called a "low point" for American women writers, the 1950s was an era dominated by male authors. Few women writers received critical praise for their work. Nevertheless, a variety of women began to bring their experiences to life in fiction, nonfiction, plays, and essays.

Until the 1950s, women writers in the United States wrote mostly about what were viewed as female themes, such as courtship and marriage. However, the fifties saw women writing not only about these themes but also about the complex ways women related to each other, as well as their ethnic and cultural experiences.

Carson McCullers wrote novels and short stories, as well as plays, essays, and some poetry. Born and raised in Savannah, Georgia, most of her works examine life in the South. One of her best-known works, *The Ballad of the Sad Café* (1951), is a collection of short stories. McCullers wrote two plays, one of which, *The Square Root of Wonderful* (1957), explores the traumatic aftermath of her husband's suicide.

Flannery O'Connor wrote novels, short stories, and essays. One of her most acclaimed novels, *Wise Blood*, was published in 1952. A book of short stories called *A Good Man Is Hard to Find and Other Stories* was published in 1955. Born and raised in the South, her works take place in southern settings and her themes revolve around race, poverty, and religion.

Anne Morrow Lindbergh was the widow of world-famous aviator Charles Lindbergh. In 1927 Charles Lindbergh became the first person to fly solo across the Atlantic Ocean. Anne herself was an aviation pioneer. She was the first female licensed glider pilot. She began writing in the 1930s and published more than a dozen books. Her best-known work, *Gift from the Sea* (1955), is a collection of her reflections about love, marriage, youth, and aging.

Peyton Place (1956) was one of the best-selling novels of the decade. It

> **"If I'm a lousy writer, then an awful lot of people have lousy taste."**
>
> —*author Grace Metalious, in response to criticism of her controversial novel,* **Peyton Place***, 1956*

was the first and best-known work of writer Grace Metalious. It depicts the many scandals among the inhabitants of what appears to be a serious and proper New England town. It went on to become a popular television series in the 1960s.

CARSON MCCULLERS began her career as a writer after leaving the South but continued to explore the South in her works.

GRACE METALIOUS based the setting of *Peyton Place* on three towns near where she lived in New Hampshire.

Beginning in 1956, U.S. readers became obsessed with a town called Peyton Place. Writer Grace Metalious created the world of this fictional, small New England town in the novel of the same name. "[The community of Peyton Place] was populated by characters who strive to maintain a perfect image while struggling with hypocrisy and human frailties."

The book was considered scandalous and "decent" Americans refused to read it (though many did so in secret). *Peyton Place*, which seems tame by twenty-first century standards, included subjects that were considered taboo at the time it was published: sex, profanity, alcoholism, and graphic violence. Religious leaders condemned the book and critics called it trash, but the novel quickly became a best seller. Metalious's response to her critics was simple. "If I'm a lousy writer, then an awful lot of people have lousy taste," she said in 1956. *Peyton Place* was listed on the *New York Times* best-seller list for more than a year and became an international phenomenon. A year after the 1956 publication of the book, Hollywood turned it into a movie which was also a major hit. A popular TV series in the 1960s based on the novel became the forerunner of TV dramas such as *Desperate Housewives*.

Metalious's book brought permanent and lasting changes to the publishing industry. Editors and publishers were no longer reluctant to publish novels with themes similar to those found in *Peyton Place*. Americans, in turn, no longer felt embarrassed about reading such novels in public and were encouraged to speak more openly about private struggles they were experiencing.

Lorraine Hansberry was an African American playwright. She also wrote essays, letters, and political speeches. Her family's legal battle against segregated housing in their Chicago neighborhood led her to write *A Raisin in the Sun* (1959). It became her most famous work and is still performed in theaters all over the country.

A SPIDER AND A CAT REVOLUTIONIZE READING

E. B. White wrote an endearing story of friendship between a pig named Wilbur and a spider named Charlotte in *Charlotte's Web* (1952). Critics would later call Charlotte an important literary character that represented female creativity and industriousness during an era that lacked unique female characters for children.

LORRAINE HANSBERRY'S *A RAISIN IN THE SUN* was the first play written by an African American woman to be produced on Broadway.

For generations, children had been learning to read using books called primers that featured characters named Dick, Jane, Susan, Bill, and Perky the dog. The books featured short stories, with simple sentences and words that usually had no more than two syllables. Generally referred to as Dick and Jane books, they were considered the best tools to teach children to read. A man named Theodor Seuss Geisel would forever change the way kids—and adults—read.

Better known as Dr. Seuss, Geisel wrote *The Cat in the Hat*. Its publication in 1957 revolutionized children's reading. Seuss tells the entertaining tale of a fanciful cat that amuses two children with silly tricks and brings chaos to their home. While this book used mostly one- and two-syllable words, like the Dick and Jane primers, Seuss's characters were drawn in comical fashion and readers loved the rhyming text. The book's publication made Seuss the most famous children's book author and illustrator in the world. He went on to write more than forty books.

NONFICTION DOMINATES THE DECADE

Among the most prominent nonfiction books in the fifties was a Revised Standard Version of the Bible, which led all book sales from 1952 through 1954.

73

Theodor Seuss Geisel was born on March 2, 1904, in Springfield, Massachusetts. He first began to use the name Seuss while writing for the newspaper at Dartmouth College, in New Hampshire. After graduating from Dartmouth, he attended Oxford University in Britain for a short time. He was unhappy with his studies and left Oxford to tour Europe instead. When he returned to the United States in 1927, he worked as a cartoonist. Some of his work appeared in the *Saturday Evening Post*, which was for a time the most widely circulated

DR. SEUSS sits at his drafting table in his home office in 1957. He holds one of his most famous books, *The Cat in the Hat.*

magazine in the world. Most of his work, however, was done to create advertising for an oil company. Seuss wrote and illustrated *And to Think That I Saw It on Mulberry Street*, which was published in 1937. During World War II, he made training films for the U.S. Army. After the war, he returned to writing and illustrating books.

Seuss's best-known work, *The Cat in the Hat* (1957), began as a collaboration with his publisher. An article in the May 1954 issue of *Life* magazine had claimed that U.S. children weren't learning how to read because the standard primers were boring and unimaginative. Soon after the article's publication, the publisher provided Seuss with a list of about 250 vocabulary words

from a primer. Nine months later, using 236 of the words on the list, Seuss completed *The Cat in the Hat*. The book delighted children and adults.

During the 1950s, Seuss wrote ten books. Besides *The Cat in the Hat*, Seuss's titles that decade include classics such as *Horton Hears a Who!* (1954), *How the Grinch Stole Christmas!* (1957), and *Happy Birthday to You!* (1959).

At the time of Dr. Seuss's death on September 24, 1991, he had written forty-four children's books, which had been translated into fifteen languages. His works went on to be made into eleven children's TV programs, a Broadway musical, and a motion picture.

Dr. Benjamin Spock's *The Common Sense Guide to Baby and Child Care* came in second in nonfiction book sales in the decade. Norman Vincent Peale's *The Power of Positive Thinking* (1955) inspired people to achieve success and happiness in life and business through exactly that—positive thinking. *Betty Crocker's Picture Cook Book* (1956) inspired readers to achieve success and happiness in the kitchen. James Baldwin's nonfiction work *Notes of a Native Son* (1955) addressed race relations in the United States and Europe.

■ MAD ABOUT *MAD*

Several popular magazines made their debuts in the 1950s. *Mad* is a monthly humor magazine that was founded in 1952. It satirizes (ridicules) American life, pop culture, politics, entertainment, and public figures. *Mad* made fun of backyard bomb shelters and classroom duck-and-cover drills, correctly pointing out that neither would save people from the effects of an exploded hydrogen bomb. Parents and teachers were shocked by its content. However, the magazine filled a gap in political and social satire at a time when Cold War paranoia and censorship were common, especially in the area of young adult literature. Young people loved it.

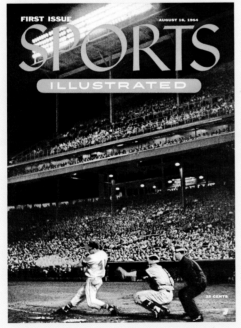

TV Guide first appeared in 1953. Its premiere issue featured a photograph of the famous comedian and actress Lucille Ball with her newborn son, Desi Arnaz Jr. For just fifteen cents per copy, Americans could either subscribe to the weekly magazine or buy it at grocery stores. People enjoyed not only the listings of TV programs but also the featured articles about their favorite TV personalities.

Sports Illustrated, the weekly sports magazine, debuted in 1954 *(left)*. In 1958, *16 Magazine* was launched. It targeted American teenagers, especially girls, and featured gossip, news, fashion tips, interviews with movie and TV stars, and sometimes included posters.

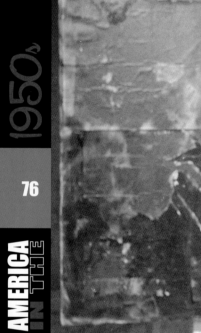

ROBERT RAUSCHENBERG sits on a sculpture in his studio in 1953 surrounded by some of his other works. Rauschenberg was a rising star in the American art scene of the 1950s.

Chapter Seven
AMERICAN SCENE:
Arts, Architecture, and Fashion in the 1950s

In the 1950s, abstract art took center stage. Pure abstract art uses forms that have no reference to how people see everyday physical reality. In other words, abstract artworks are not representations of specific scenes or things, such as landscapes or bowls of fruit. Artists of the era were more concerned with creating a new kind of experience for the viewer. Abstract painting freed itself from traditional rules of painting such as perspective, proportion, and realistic representations of the world. This allowed viewers to experience a work of art in new and sometimes challenging ways.

Jackson Pollock was at the forefront of this movement. He defied long-standing traditions of art and expanded what it meant for artists to express themselves through their paintings. Using a stick, Pollock dripped paint onto the canvas or sometimes splattered it directly from a can to create seemingly random patterns. Many people did not understand Pollock's work and labeled him Jack the Dripper. Pollock defended his paintings, saying, "It's just like looking at a bed of flowers. You don't tear your hair out over what it means."

Despite criticism, Pollock's 18-foot-wide (5 m) *Blue Poles*, painted in 1952, drew widespread approval from many art critics. His importance as an artist continued to grow. Pollock's wife, Lee Krasner, was also an abstract

AMERICA IN THE 1950s

Born in Port Arthur, Texas, in 1925, Robert Rauschenberg found his true calling as an artist after serving in World War II. Studying under the GI bill—which provided American soldiers with money for a college education—Rauschenberg first studied in Paris, France, then in North Carolina. But it was in New York City that he found his artistic voice. The work of fellow artists and the vivid imagery of city life made their mark on his work, especially on the collages that brought him fame. A collage consists of cutting and pasting together assorted images to create a new piece.

A highly experimental German artistic movement called Dada embraced this technique in the 1920s and 1930s and established it as a distinct visual art. Influenced by Dada, Rauschenberg created a unique collage-style through a bold use of three-dimensional objects. *Monogram* (1955–1959) is a prime example: it incorporates a tire, a stuffed goat, and a painting. The relationship among unrelated objects created a dramatically new understanding of imagery. Rauschenberg dubbed these types of work "combines," for the way they combined unrelated images to create something new.

Rauschenberg went on to found Experiments in Art and Technology (E.A.T.), a nonprofit organization that teamed artists and engineers in creative environments. In the 1980s, he started the Rauschenberg Overseas Cultural Interchange (ROCI) to promote "world peace and understanding" through art. It is, however, his work with combines in the 1950s that established him as an original visionary in art. Rauschenberg died in 2008, and his works are displayed in museums around the world.

expressionist. She painted *Cool White*, one of her best-known works, in 1959.

Like Pollock, artist Robert Rauschenberg was also interested in challenging artistic norms. He created some of his artworks with paint. But he also used found objects such as parts of ladders, automobile tires, rags, Coca-Cola bottles, old radios, and newspaper clippings to create "combines," his term for pieces that combined painting and sculpture. Rauschenberg's combines merge artistic expression with items from daily life. The overall effect is that

"It's just like looking at a bed of flowers. You don't tear your hair out over what it means."

—artist Jackson Pollock, commenting on his paintings, 1952

the viewer sees everyday objects in a new way.

What Rauschenberg did for everyday objects, Jasper Johns did for everyday symbols. Johns became well known for works such as *Flag* (1955), which took the U.S. flag out of its context as a national symbol and showed it to viewers as an item in and of itself. Johns provided viewers with a way to look at the symbols around them without "intended meaning" dictating what the viewer sees. Johns was extremely successful early in his career. His painting *False Start* (1959) sold for $80 million, making it the most expensive painting ever sold by a living artist.

JASPER JOHNS PAINTED *FLAG* in 1955.

Abstractionist sculptors made their art out of various materials and experimented with new shapes. By hammering, twisting, or welding steel and bronze, sculptors formed unique, nonrepresentational sculptures that captured the imagination. Already an established artist by the 1950s, Alexander Calder was known for creating hanging sculptures that moved, known as mobiles. In the 1950s, he turned his attention to monumental sculptures, creating pieces such as *.125* for the John F. Kennedy International Airport terminal in New York City.

As modern art gained a following, representational artists continued to find success among the public of the 1950s. Among them were Andrew Wyeth, Georgia O'Keeffe, and Anna "Grandma" Moses. Moses's paintings are considered to be representative of folk art, or works by a person without any formal training. The works reflect the world around the artist as he or she sees it. Grandma Moses's paintings were very popular, starting in the mid-forties through the fifties, and were reproduced on fabrics, china, and greeting cards.

■ COLOR FIELD

Color field painting developed in New York City during the 1940s and 1950s. Closely related to abstract art, color field is characterized by large fields, or areas, of flat, solid color spread across the canvas. The result is an unbroken surface and a flat picture plane.

Workers install **ALEXANDER CALDER'S** *.125* at John F. Kennedy International Airport in New York City in 1957.

MARK ROTHKO PAINTED *NO. 13* IN 1958. It shows red and white bars of color on a yellow background.

Emphasis was placed on overall form and process, instead of brushstrokes and action. By the late 1950s, formats of stripes, targets, simple geometric patterns, and landscape and nature images were common. Mark Rothko, Clyfford Still, Barnett Newman, and Robert Motherwell were among the most noted color field painters.

■ PHOTOGRAPHY: *THE FAMILY OF MAN*

By the 1950s, photography had become an accepted art form. In 1955 a photography exhibit called *The Family of Man* debuted at the Museum of Modern Art in New York City. More than five hundred photographs by 273 photographers from sixty-eight countries were chosen from among two million pictures. The exhibit represented the human experience, reflecting themes of birth, love, joy, war, illness, and death, all transcending racial, social, and cultural barriers. At a time when Cold War tensions separated countries, the goal of the exhibit was to show that peoples throughout the world—no matter how different—experience life in many similar ways. The exhibit traveled to thirty-eight countries, attracting an estimated nine million viewers.

■ COMICS TICKLE AMERICANS' FUNNY BONES

Comic strips continued to make American newspaper readers chuckle in the 1950s. American innovation in the field of comics saw the 1950s debut some of the most popular comic strips in the world.

For example, *Beetle Bailey* is set on a U.S. Army military post. Created by Mort Walker, it first appeared in newspapers on September 4, 1950. World War II vets could relate to the lighter side of army life as they read the funnies in the morning paper. The strip went on to find an even broader spectrum of appeal. In the early twenty-first century, it is one of the only comics still written and drawn by its creator.

Hi and Lois, a comic strip about a suburban family, was also created by Mort Walker, with illustrations by Dik Browne. It first appeared in American newspapers on October 18, 1954. The strip follows a wholesome "nuclear family," a phrase that represents the 1950s American ideal of Mom, Dad, two kids, a dog, and a station wagon. In the 2000s, *Hi and Lois* is still popular, and Mort Walker's two sons write and draw the strip for newspapers across the country.

Another long-running comic strip that got its start in the 1950s is *Dennis the Menace*, which first appeared in newspapers on March 12, 1951. Hank Ketchum created the comic world of young Dennis, his family, his neighbors, and friends. Ketchum's own four-year-old son was the inspiration for Dennis. In the comic, Dennis is a good-natured kid who inadvertently torments his cranky older neighbor, Mr. Wilson. Readers enjoy Dennis's mischief while also responding to his upbeat and innocent personality.

CARTOONIST CHARLES SCHULZ drew, wrote, and colored *Peanuts*, which was syndicated in 1950.

American innovation in the field of comics saw the 1950s debut some of the most popular comic strips in the world.

Marmaduke debuted in 1954. Created by Brad Anderson, the comic revolves around the Winslow family and their Great Dane dog, Marmaduke. The lovable dog and his devoted owners are still entertaining fans in the twenty-first century.

B.C. was created in 1958. Johnny Hart wrote and drew the comic for nearly fifty years. Set in prehistoric times, it features a group of cavemen and animals that include a bird, a dinosaur, and a snake. The strip was quite quirky and sometimes expressed Hart's religious views. It became a staple of the funnies page and continues in the 2000s under the hand of Hart's daughter and grandson.

The most influential comic strip to debut in the 1950s is Charles Schulz's *Peanuts*. Schulz used the common comic-strip theme of children to express deeper human sentiments. Charlie Brown, for example, was a voice for Charles Schulz's own melancholy. Pals Lucy, Linus, Snoopy, and the gang dealt with a range of emotions more complex than those of other cartoon characters of the time.

■ THE 1950s SKYLINE: ARCHITECTURE

The 1950s saw remarkable architectural accomplishments. For example, the four-building world headquarters of the United Nations in New York City was designed by a team of eleven architects, led by American architect Wallace K. Harrison. Richard Neutra created the Hinds House in Los Angeles, California, in 1952 and the Navy Chapel at Miramar, California, in 1956. In 1953 Buckminster Fuller designed the Ford Rotunda in Dearborn, Michigan, and the Mini-Earth Sphere Geoscope in Ithaca, New York. The Geoscope is a structure intended to expand visitors' comprehension of their position on "Spaceship Earth," as Fuller called it. It contains a large model of Earth, upon which beams of light indicate changing statistics such as human migration, population density, weather patterns, and even weapons buildups. Fuller's goal in creating the Geoscope was to create "livingry," or tools to aid humanity, instead of destructive weaponry.

83

Eero Saarinen was a Finnish American architect and furniture designer. He was famous for varying styles—simple sweeping, arching, or straight lines. Saarinen designed a steel-and-glass building for General Motors in Michigan and the headquarters of a number of American corporations, including John Deere in Illinois and CBS television in New York City. Throughout the 1950s, Saarinen designed the campus buildings for several major American universities, including Vassar in New York and Yale in Connecticut.

Frank Lloyd Wright was the most prominent architect of the fifties. In 1951 Wright designed both the First Unitarian Meeting House in Madison, Wisconsin, and the Wayfarers Chapel in Palos Verdes, California. He drew the plans for the Price Tower in Bartlesville, Oklahoma, in 1955. In 1959 he drew the plans for both the Beth Shalom Synagogue in Elkins Park, Pennsylvania, and the Kalita Humphreys Theater in Dallas, Texas.

Perhaps Wright's most notable achievement in the 1950s was the Solomon R. Guggenheim Museum on New York City's Fifth Avenue. It was begun in 1958 and completed in 1959, after Wright's death. A conch shell inspired Wright's design for the museum's exhibition galleries. Shaped like a large cone, it includes a sloping ramp that spirals down for seven stories beneath a huge glass dome.

THE GUGGENHEIM MUSEUM has been a draw for New Yorkers and visitors since it opened in 1959.

■ INSIDE A 1950s CLOSET

Women's clothes of the decade ranged from the hooded dress (made of a single tube of hip-clinging knit fabric) to a skirt worn over a stiff crinoline petticoat to give fullness to the skirt. Hats and gloves were required for many social functions and for attending religious services.

In the early 1950s, Italian shoe-makers created the skinny-heeled shoes called stilettos. *Stiletto* means "little dagger" in Italian. Most stilettos were not more than 3 inches (8 cm) high. When female movie stars such as Marilyn Monroe, Jayne Mansfield, and Sophia Loren wore them, the shoes' popularity exploded. As early as 1953, concerns surfaced that the heels could cause problems for the wearer. These problems included falls, poor posture, and foot, ankle, and knee injuries. Nevertheless, when French clothing designer Christian Dior teamed his dresses with stilettos in 1957, many American women loved the look.

THESE TWO WOMEN have embraced the 1950s look of dresses and stilettos.

Girls of the 1950s often wore rolled-up jeans with casual blouses or men's shirts. A felt skirt on which a poodle design was appliquéd was another favorite. Girls' hairstyles ranged from the ponytail and poodle cut to the bouffant look, with most of the hair puffed up on top of the head.

Mamie Doud Eisenhower was born in Iowa in 1896. Her family moved to Colorado when she was a child, and she was educated in Denver, the state's capital. Mamie met Ike Eisenhower in Texas in 1915, and they were married less than a year later. She gave birth to the first of the couple's two sons in 1917. Affectionately called Litty Icky, Doud Dwight died in 1921, at the age of three. Mamie and Ike never fully recovered from the loss, but they were determined to move on with their lives. A second son, John, was born in 1922.

Mamie was known for her bright blue eyes and creamy complexion. She was considered a charming and gracious hostess who possessed genuine warmth and sincere concern for others. After her husband became president in 1953, Mamie was a popular first lady. She appeared on the "Most Admired Women" lists in popular magazines every year until her death.

Mamie was fascinated by clothes and fashion all her life. Despite being a grandmother in her fifties by the time she was living in the White House, she was determined to project a stylish and youthful image to the public. She succeeded. Many American women loved her because she seemed to be just like them. She famously wore a hairstyle that included bangs, which were uncommon in the fifties. When photos of what became known as the Mamie

MAMIE EISENHOWER popularized pearl chokers and button-earrings, as well as hair cuts with bangs.

Look were published, thousands of women rushed to get their hair cut the same way. Her style prompted women to get copies of her famous accessories: pearl chokers, button earrings, charm bracelets, glittery pins, and fitted hats.

When Ike left the presidency, the couple spent quiet days on their farm in Pennsylvania. Ike died in 1969. After suffering a stroke in September 1979, Mamie died on November 1. She continues to be remembered as one of America's most influential and best-loved first ladies.

As the 1950s continued, many girls and women began wearing two-piece bikini swimsuits. Bikinis were considered very daring at the time. Some parents and many religious leaders called them scandalous and far too revealing.

Businessmen wore suits, ties, and hats to and from the office. On weekends they shed their formal attire for colorful sport shirts and slacks or jeans. The favorite casual dress of high school boys was either baggy pegged pants or denim jeans with rolled-up cuffs. Both T-shirts and sport shirts were regular attire. In 1955 teenage boys joined college men in what became known as the pink revolution. They donned pink shirts and pink striped or polka-dot ties. At school dances, it was hard to find any young men not wearing pink with their gray flannel suits. Hairstyles ranged from the flattop and crew cut, which had been popular in the wartime 1940s, to the swooping ducktail cut worn by superstar Elvis Presley.

■ PUSHING FASHION BOUNDARIES

In the offbeat beatnik scene, women wore mostly black. Rejecting loose-fitting pants and blouses, women favored formfitting pants and tops. The tight clothing accentuated the wearer's body and her femininity.

Another nonconformist fashion trend was the "greaser" look. Popularized by Elvis Presley, this fashion trend started among working-class youths and motorcycle clubs such as the Hell's Angels. After Elvis introduced it to the mainstream, however, guys with thickly greased-back hair, leather jackets, and tight jeans were seen in high schools all over the country. This style was a precursor to many punk trends that would later crop up in the mid-1970s and 1980s.

BIKINIS pushed the boundaries of what was considered appropriate swimwear in the 1950s.

A family sits in their living room watching a children's show on
TELEVISION in the 1950s. TV reached new heights of popularity
in the 1950s.

Chapter Eight

STARS SHINE:

On Stage and Screen in the 1950s

Although experimental television broadcasts were being made as early as the 1920s, it was not until well after World War II that the TV industry really came to life. A national poll in 1945 found that only 19 percent of Americans had actually seen a television show. As late as 1947, TV manufacturers produced fewer than 200,000 televisions a year. By contrast, in the 1950s, manufacturers turned out 6 million to 7 million TVs a year.

At the start of the 1950s, only a small number of U.S. cities had more than one television station. Networks would sometimes combine their programming to bring popular events such as the World Series or a heavyweight boxing championship to a large audience.

The obstacle to nationwide television was technical: TV signals do not bend and cannot travel far. The curvature of Earth's surface prevented television receivers across the country from picking up all but local signals. Because of this, program directors were limited to showing local programs. This problem was solved in 1951 when a coaxial cable (a tube containing a central electrical conductor surrounded by material that transmits high-frequency signals) was stretched across the United States. The first coast-to-coast television broadcast was President Truman's speech at the Japanese Peace Treaty Conference on September 4, 1951. Ninety-four stations broadcast the speech to 40 million viewers across the country.

TELEVISION TAKES CENTER STAGE

Some people criticized TV, calling it the idiot box, because they saw little value in most TV programs. They also objected to television violence. It was estimated that in the year 1954 alone, more people were murdered on TV than the United States lost in the entire Korean War.

The critics, however, were far outnumbered by the many Americans who enjoyed TV programs. They didn't want to miss one minute of their favorite shows. Historian David Halberstam said, "Studies showed that when a popular program was on, toilets flushed all over certain cities, as if on cue, during commercials or the moment the program was over."

The television revolution caused significant lifestyle changes. Viewers tended to stay up later at night and leave home less often. Restaurants were more crowded during early evening hours, so people could get back to the "tube" for the nighttime shows. Products advertised on TV, such as refrigerators and washing machines, soared in public acceptance. With the appearance of the portable TV dinner in 1954, families began to eat their evening meal in front of the television set. Dinnertime conversation became a lost art in some families.

Radio programs and motion pictures were hit hard by the power of television. Many movie theaters began to close because attendance fell off sharply. In New York City, 55 movie theaters had closed by 1951. In the same year in Southern California, 134 movie theaters closed their doors as a result of competition from television.

> Some people criticized TV, calling it the idiot box, because they saw little value in most TV programs.

THE ZANY COMEDIANS

Milton Berle became television's first superstar. From his first appearance on TV in 1948, he caused his audiences to howl with laughter. On his show, *Texaco Star Theater*, he brought singing, dancing, music, and comedy into the family living room. Berle was so famous that he appeared on the covers of both *Time* and *Newsweek* in the same week. It was common for TV stations to delay coverage of the day's news until Berle's program ended.

MILTON BERLE *(center)* portrays Queen Cleopatra in a skit on his TV show with *(from left)* comedian Jack Benny and actors Laurence Harvey, Kirk Douglas, and Charlton Heston in the late 1950s.

For four years starting in 1950, *Your Show of Shows* entertained countless American television viewers. The program featured comedians Sid Caesar and Imogene Coca. Caesar and Coca were known for their spoofs of popular movies.

The Honeymooners starred Jackie Gleason as a cranky but lovable bus driver. The TV program also starred Audrey Meadows as Gleason's outspoken wife; Art Carney as Norton, their oddball neighbor; and Joyce Randolph as Norton's wife, Trixie. The show aired on CBS from 1955 to 1956. In the 2000s, it can still be seen in reruns and is considered a TV classic.

Radio had been the chief form of home entertainment before the emergence of TV. Soon some of radio's stellar comedians turned their talents to television. *The Colgate Comedy Hour* boasted hosts such as Eddie Cantor, Bud Abbott and Lou Costello, and Dean Martin and Jerry Lewis. Other TV shows featured Jack Benny, Red Skelton, Jimmy Durante, and the married comedy duo George Burns and Gracie Allen.

Newspaper columnist Ed Sullivan became the host of television's *Toast of the Town*, a popular variety show in 1955. It featured comedy acts, magicians, athletes, and singers, including Elvis Presley. There were so many different types of performers that audiences everywhere tuned in with great anticipation to see what acts Sullivan would feature next.

The biggest comedy hit by far of the 1950s was *I Love Lucy*, which premiered on October 15, 1951. One of the most beloved television shows of all time, it featured wacky comedian Lucille Ball and her Cuban-born bandleader husband, Desi Arnaz, as Lucy and Ricky Ricardo. Vivian Vance and William Frawley rounded out the cast as the Ricardos' friends and landlords, Ethel and Fred Mertz. At the end of its first month, *I Love Lucy* displaced Milton Berle's *Texaco Star Theater* as the top-rated TV program. Less than a year later, its stars signed a new contract totaling $8 million, which at that time was the largest amount paid to any television performers. More people watched *I Love Lucy* in January 1953 than saw President Eisenhower's televised inauguration that same month. By 1954 more than 50 million of the nation's 152 million people—or an astounding one-third of the total population—were the funny foursome's devoted fans.

From left: Actresses Vivian Vance and Lucille Ball and actors Desi Arnaz and William Frawley compete in a tuna-fishing contest on an episode of ***I LOVE LUCY*** first aired in 1956.

Lucille Ball (1911–1989) was born and raised in Jamestown, New York. She dropped out of high school at the age of fifteen and moved to New York City to study acting and work as an actress. By the mid-1930s, she was living in Hollywood and had appeared in dozens of movies.

Beginning in 1951, she starred in television's *I Love Lucy* alongside her husband, Desi Arnaz. Already well known, she became one of the most popular actresses in the country. She and Arnaz founded Desilu Studios, which produced *I Love Lucy*. The studio went on to produce popular TV shows such as *My Three Sons*, *Star Trek*, and *Mission: Impossible*.

After *I Love Lucy* ended its run in 1957, Ball and Arnaz divorced, and Ball became the president of Desilu. She went on to star in a few other sitcoms, always as a divorced woman. Her strong, independent characters paved the way for the success of future female comedians and actresses, such as Carol Burnett and Mary Tyler Moore. Ball herself is remembered as one of the most talented performers in TV history.

One of the first Hispanics to be seen regularly on television, Desi Arnaz (1917–1986) was a talented actor, singer, and musician—and a pioneer in the television industry. Born in Santiago, Cuba, in 1917, Arnaz immigrated to Miami, Florida, in 1935.

In the early 1950s, sitcoms were not performed before live audiences and only one camera recorded all the action. Arnaz and Karl Freund, a cameraman who worked on *I Love Lucy*, pioneered the idea of staging the show as a play in front of a live audience. That way, the audience's laughter could be heard along with the dialogue. Arnaz and Freund also decided to film the show using three or four cameras, so the same scene could be shown from different angles. Arnaz started the practice of warming up the studio audience before the show began by telling jokes.

A brilliant businessman, Arnaz arranged for Desilu to control all the rights to the *I Love Lucy* episodes. This made it possible for Arnaz and Ball to profit from reruns of the series. Arnaz's arrangement is considered one of the shrewdest deals in television history. His foresight in filming techniques and in retaining ownership of the shows he produced resulted in practices that became common in the television industry.

93

A unique problem arose in 1952, when Lucille Ball became pregnant with the couple's second child. In those times, pregnant women were not commonly seen on television or in films because this was considered to be in poor taste. Actors were not allowed to use the word "pregnant," so words such as "expecting" were used instead. Lucy's pregnancy, however, became part of the program's story line.

The episode in which Lucy gave birth first aired on January 19, 1953. The air date coincided with Ball's real-life delivery of Desi Arnaz Jr. For years the episode held the record as the most watched TV program of all time. A whopping 68 percent of all the televisions in America were tuned in to the episode. In the 2000s, *I Love Lucy* can still be seen in reruns and is considered one of television's classic programs.

■ FAMILY FARE FOR MANY TASTES

In the 1950s, almost everyone could find something interesting to watch on television. For fans of spectacular programs, the top attraction of the decade was *Peter Pan*, the first television broadcast of a Broadway production. It was said that one out of every two Americans watched this program.

Beginning in 1952, *Ozzie and Harriet* was the country's favorite family show. It featured scripts written by Ozzie Nelson that were drawn from and acted by his real-life family. The program ran for fourteen seasons. Among the other popular family shows of the era were *Father Knows Best*, *Our Miss Brooks*, *Make Room for Daddy*, and *Leave It to Beaver*.

The cast of *LEAVE IT TO BEAVER* poses for a family portrait in 1957. Beaver was portrayed by Jerry Mathers *(lower right)*.

Quiz shows became a TV phenomenon in the 1950s. Americans were fascinated by the idea of ordinary people winning instant riches. Popular big-money quiz shows included *You Bet Your Life*, *What's My Line?*, *The $64,000 Question*, and *Twenty-One*.

Twenty-One attracted a large audience but suffered a scandalous fate. On the show, two players competed against each other to score twenty-one points by answering questions. The questions increased in difficulty, so they were worth increasing amounts of money.

Charles Van Doren was a handsome young university instructor who appeared on *Twenty-One* in 1956. He amazed 25 million viewers a week with his ability to answer difficult questions. Van Doren earned a record payoff of $129,000 and became a celebrity. His fame turned to shame when Herbert Stempel, a college student who had competed against Van Doren and won

$49,500 on the show, revealed a shocking secret. Stempel told the press that all the contestants were given the correct answers in advance and were allowed to win money until their popularity waned. He told reporters that the entire show was a fake. Stempel wanted revenge because the producers of *Twenty-One* had ordered him to give a wrong answer so that he would lose to Van Doren.

At first, Van Doren denied the charges. However, on November 2, 1959, he confessed that the show was indeed a fraud. Van Doren deeply regretted his role in the scandal and was not prosecuted for his misdeeds. Some contestants on *The $64,000 Question* and other quiz shows also admitted that they had been given answers in advance. Soon the big-money quiz shows faded from TV screens. When they were resurrected for new audiences in the late twentieth century, they were closely monitored to maintain the fairness of the questions and the integrity of the contestants.

CHARLES VAN DOREN *(left)* faces off against HERBERT STEMPEL *(right)* on the quiz show *Twenty-One*. Host Jack Barry poses the questions.

These shows portrayed parent-centered, white, middle-class families where problems were often solved more quickly and easily than in real life. Nevertheless, many families aspired to be like the families they saw on TV.

Fans of Westerns had many programs to choose from. These included *Gunsmoke*, *King of the Cowboys*, and *Zorro*, featuring a mysterious avenger of evil deeds, who left only a telltale *Z* to mark his passing. Other popular television Westerns were *Wyatt Earp*; *Have Gun, Will Travel*; *The Rifleman*; *Wagon Train*; *The Cisco Kid*; and *Cheyenne*. Westerns were such a hit that one actor observed, "If Shakespeare were alive today, he'd be writing Westerns."

Dragnet was TV's most widely watched detective program. Creator Jack Webb not only directed the show and wrote many of its scripts but also starred in the show. *Perry Mason* and *Alfred Hitchcock Presents* were other popular mystery and suspense programs.

The 1950s provided some of the best live plays ever written for television. They were one-time performances that were broadcast live. These hour-long shows were featured on such programs as *Philco Playhouse*, *Kraft Television Theater*, and the *U.S. Steel Hour*.

Paddy Chayefsky's TV play *Marty* (1953), about a lonely, awkward man, was a smashing success. Chayefsky later expanded his hour-long script into

DICK CLARK *(top right)* **HOSTED TELEVISION'S** *AMERICAN BANDSTAND* from 1957 until the end of its run in the late 1980s.

a full-length film. The film, starring Ernest Borgnine as Marty, won the 1955 Academy Award for best picture.

Rod Serling's *Requiem for a Heavyweight* was performed on the live show *Playhouse 90* in 1956. The play tells the story of a defeated boxer who believes he has nothing left except his own self-respect. This moving study of human emotions is considered one of the three greatest prizefight movies ever made.

Music also had a place on television. In 1951 *Amahl and the Night Visitors*, by Gian Carlo Menotti, became the first opera ever written for television. For the latest hits, disc jockey Dick Clark on *American Bandstand* had 20 million regular viewers and kept teenagers dancing—both on the show and in their living rooms. Van Cliburn played the piano masterfully on television. Many singers of popular songs also lent their talents to the tube.

Television did not overlook its youngest viewers. Children's shows included the popular *Kukla, Fran and Ollie*; *Captain Kangaroo*; *Howdy Doody*; and *Mighty Mouse Playhouse*. *Lassie*, named for the dog that captured the hearts of nearly every youngster who watched her perform, was a favorite show among children and adults. And thousands of boys wore coonskin caps in tribute to their television hero, Davy Crockett, from the program of the same name. The TV show was based on the real-life Crockett, a nineteenth-century American frontiersman and politician.

■ NEWS, PUBLIC EVENTS, AND POLITICS

TV news programs in the early 1950s lasted only fifteen minutes, but later, they were extended to half an hour. Television news coverage became a living newspaper. For the first time in history, American viewers could actually see and hear the daily headlines at home. Soon most Americans were relying more on television than on newspapers and radio for news.

The major news commentators of the 1950s were David Brinkley and Chet Huntley at NBC, an ABC team headed by John Daly, and Edward R. Murrow at CBS. Murrow was already well known for his outstanding radio broadcasts from Europe during World War II. In 1951 he launched a popular TV news show called *See It Now*, in which he covered events all over the world. Murrow said, "No journalistic age was ever given a weapon for truth with quite the scope of this fledgling television."

Important public events also were covered on television. Viewers saw Senator Estes Kefauver's congressional hearings on organized crime in 1950 and the coronation of Britain's Queen Elizabeth II in 1952. When Soviet leader Nikita Khrushchev made an unprecedented visit to the United States in 1959, television cameras were there.

Television played an important role in the 1952 presidential election. Viewers watched the political conventions, as well as some of the speeches of candidates Dwight D. Eisenhower and Adlai Stevenson. For the first time, a barrage of short political advertisements took aim at TV viewers. These ads began to influence voters' opinions.

EDWARD R. MURROW
(left) interviews a U.S. Marine in Korea for *See It Now*.

> ❝No journalistic age was ever given a weapon for truth with quite the scope of this fledgling television.❞

—*Edward R. Murrow, host of* See It Now, *1952*

■ AT THE MOVIES

Hollywood tried various innovations to win back at least part of the huge audience it had lost to television. The search for technological improvements began in 1952 with the introduction of Cinerama. Cinerama used three projectors pointed at a large screen. It made viewers feel that they were in the middle of the action. But the expense of redesigning theaters with extra-wide screens and acquiring the necessary equipment limited Cinerama's possibilities.

Next came three-dimensional (3-D) movies, which used two projectors. Audiences watched 3-D films with glasses that gave the illusion of depth. However, most 3-D films were poorly scripted adventure stories. This fad soon faded in popularity, to be revived in the 1990s and 2000s.

Producers at Twentieth Century Fox movie studios decided to gamble with a new projection method. Called Cinemascope, it showed nearly twice as much image in each frame. (It was a precursor to modern wide-screen movies.) Released in 1953, *The Robe*, a story about what might have happened to a robe worn by Jesus Christ, was the first Cinemascope film. It was a huge box-office success. So was *The Ten Commandments* (1956), a biography of Moses, the man who led the Jews out of Egypt thousands of years ago. *Ben-Hur* (1959) was the most colossal of the Cinemascope epics. Charlton Heston starred as a Jewish patriot during the early days of Christianity. This extravagant movie was filmed on more than three hundred sets with ten thousand extras, one hundred thousand costumes, and one million props. Costing $15 million—the most expensive movie ever made to that time—it earned more than $80 million and won eleven Academy Awards.

Science-fiction films were popular in the fifties too. *Destination Moon* (1950) was the first major movie about the possibility of lunar exploration, shown nineteen years before this spectacular mission was actually accomplished. In *The Day the Earth Stood Still* (1951), an alien spaceman and a robot land in Washington, D.C., in a flying saucer. Unless humans obey the spaceman's order to stop using atomic bombs, the robot will use those weapons to destroy Earth. Other major science-fiction movies were *Invasion of the Body Snatchers* (1956), *The Incredible Shrinking Man* (1957), and *On the Beach* (1959). Many of these movies reflected the public's fear of nuclear destruction.

Film noir, French for "black film," describes a kind of Hollywood drama that was very popular in the 1940s and 1950s. The movies ranged from crime thrillers to "message movies," which focused on societal issues such as McCarthyism and racism. The most notable film noirs from the 1950s include Alfred Hitchcock's *Strangers on a Train* (1951); *Kiss Me Deadly* (1955), based on a novel by Mickey Spillane; and Orson Welles's *Touch of Evil* (1958).

Sensational new movie stars hit the screen in the 1950s. Marilyn Monroe topped the list. She achieved worldwide fame as a blonde bombshell in *Gentlemen Prefer Blondes* (1953). Her huge box-office hits also included *The Seven Year Itch* (1955), *Bus Stop* (1956), and *Some Like It Hot* (1959).

Elizabeth Taylor was a popular child star in the 1940s. Her career continued to grow in the 1950s. In 1951's *A Place in the Sun*, the seventeen-year-old violet-eyed beauty played a pampered society girl whose romance with a handsome poor man ends in catastrophe. Taylor also was praised for her performances in *Giant* (1956) and *Cat on a Hot Tin Roof* (1958).

The most regal of the new female stars, Grace Kelly brought sophistication and elegance to the movie screen. British director Alfred Hitchcock worked with her in three classic film thrillers: *Dial M for Murder* and *Rear Window*, both in 1954, and *To Catch a Thief* (1955). But it was her role as a dowdy, working-class wife in *The Country Girl* (1954) that earned her an Academy Award for best actress.

Marlon Brando achieved fame as an actor in the 1950s. He had starred as hotheaded construction worker Stanley Kowalski in *A Streetcar Named Desire* on the Broadway stage and in 1951 performed the same role on the movie screen. Brando went on to make several other box-office hits in the 1950s. These included *Viva Zapata* (1952), *The*

Wild One (1953), *On the Waterfront* and *Desiree* (1954), *Guys and Dolls* (1955), *The Teahouse of the August Moon* (1956), *Sayonara* (1957), and *The Young Lions* (1958).

James Dean had a brief but spectacular movie career as an actor in the 1950s. In 1955 alone, this handsome, moody Indiana farm boy starred in three films. All had enormous appeal to teenagers: *East of Eden*, *Rebel Without a Cause*, and *Giant*. A week after he completed *Giant*, Dean died in a car crash. His death "enshrined him forever as the idol and symbol of a restless, confused, but fundamentally idealistic younger generation."

GRACE KELLY AND MARLON BRANDO pose with their Oscars after her win for best actress in *The Country Girl* and his for best actor in *On the Waterfront* at the 1954 Academy Awards.

Besides the newcomers, Hollywood's veteran actors made some outstanding movies in the fifties. Gary Cooper starred in *High Noon* (1952), believed by some movie historians to be the best Western movie ever made. An aging Gloria Swanson starred in *Sunset Boulevard* (1950). Bette Davis starred in *All About Eve* (1950), and Judy Garland was superb in *A Star Is Born* (1954). Katharine Hepburn and Humphrey Bogart were perfectly matched in *The African Queen* (1951), a story about a rough riverboat captain and the proper British lady who is his only passenger.

■ ON THE STAGE

Popular live theater in the 1950s included splashy musicals and serious plays. Many of the productions first staged in that decade are still being enjoyed in the twenty-first century.

Guys and Dolls (1950) was the first smash musical hit of the decade. The next year, Broadway audiences raved about Richard Rodgers and Oscar Hammerstein's *The King and I*. *My Fair Lady* was the biggest musical hit of the decade. It opened in 1956 and had 2,717 consecutive performances, breaking all previous records for Broadway musicals. Meredith Willson's *The Music Man* (1957) delighted Broadway theatergoers. Based on Shakespeare's *Romeo and*

MY FAIR LADY wowed Broadway in the 1950s. It starred Julie Andrews as Eliza Doolittle and Rex Harrison as Professor Henry Higgins.

Juliet, *West Side Story* opened in 1957. The last great musical of the decade was Rodgers and Hammerstein's *The Sound of Music* (1959). All of these theatrical musicals went on to become film hits.

Some outstanding nonmusical plays also debuted in the fifties. New playwright William Inge provided four plays that drew large audiences: *Come Back, Little Sheba* and *Picnic* (1953), *Bus Stop* (1954), and *The Dark at the Top of the Stairs* (1957). Playwright Tennessee Williams's work, *The Rose Tattoo*, won a Tony Award, Broadway's highest honor, for best play, in 1952. His play, *Cat on a Hot Tin Roof*, won a Pulitzer Prize for Drama in 1955. Both plays, as well as a third Williams hit, *Sweet Bird of Youth* (1958), drew large audiences and later went on to make a mark in film history.

Arthur Miller's *The Crucible* was first performed onstage in 1953. Set in colonial times, it chronicles the hysteria that overtakes a New England town when young girls accuse their neighbors of being witches. It was widely considered to be a commentary on the anti-Communist hysteria that was gripping the nation at that time. That same year, John Patrick's *The Teahouse of the August Moon* was staged.

Inherit the Wind, the story of the 1925 landmark Scopes trial that revolved around the teaching of evolution in public schools, opened in 1955. That same year, *The Diary of Anne Frank* was another powerful play. It tells the famous story of a Jewish teenager whose family hid from the Nazis in Amsterdam, the Netherlands, during World War II.

Eugene O'Neill's drama, *Long Day's Journey into Night*, premiered in 1956, after his death. That same year, Patrick Dennis's novel *Auntie Mame* was adapted for Broadway, starring Rosalind Russell in the title role. *Look Homeward, Angel*, based on Thomas Wolfe's powerful novel of the same name, was first performed in 1957. *Sunrise at Campobello*, the story of President Franklin D. Roosevelt's fight against polio, premiered in 1958. The next year, audiences saw a play about another person overcoming physical difficulties: Helen Keller, who was blind and deaf. *The Miracle Worker* told Keller's life story. Also in 1959, Lorraine Hansberry's groundbreaking novel about an African American family in Chicago, *A Raisin in the Sun*, reached Broadway.

1950s

AMERICA IN THE

Chapter Nine

"ROCK AROUND THE CLOCK":
Music in the 1950s

Popular music in the early 1950s was much as it had been in the previous decade. Romantic ballads by such vocalists as Perry Como, Eddie Fisher, Harry Belafonte, Nat King Cole, Patti Page, Kay Starr, Teresa Brewer, Rosemary Clooney, and the Andrews Sisters blanketed the nation.

■ "ALL ABOARD": RHYTHM AND BLUES

Rhythm and blues music started in the early 1900s but found new popularity with the arrival of a variety of musicians and a record label called Motown. Blues music got its name because its songs focused on bad luck, hard times, and personal and financial trouble. Repetitive rhythms repeated the sorrowful chants and conveyed the singer's sadness.

In northern cities such as Chicago and Detroit, musicians Muddy Waters, Willie Dixon, John Lee Hooker, Howlin' Wolf, and Elmore James were among those who played what was known as Mississippi Delta blues. They were backed by bass drums, piano, and sometimes the harmonica. Songs such as "All Aboard" and "Goin' Down Louisiana" became hits. At the same time, performers in the South, including T-Bone Walker and B. B. King, were pioneers in a style of guitar music that combined jazz and the blues. Their hits included "You Know I Love You" and "Bad Luck."

African American songwriter Berry Gordy became a record producer in the early 1950s. He sought to sign other African Americans to his record label—Motown Records (named after "motor town," or Detroit, home of major auto manufacturers)—which he founded in 1959. His goal was to bring African American music to white audiences for greater cultural acceptance and for greater success. In the late 1950s, Gordy signed a group called Smokey Robinson and the Miracles.

After the group had a number-one hit in 1960, Motown went on to become one of the best-known labels in music history. Gordy's success helped advance not only rhythm and blues music but also black singers and songwriters.

■ "GROOVIN' HIGH": JAZZ AND BEBOP

Jazz music began in black communities in the South in the early 1900s. It fuses African and European music styles and allows for a great deal of improvisation. Jazz instruments typically included the saxophone, trumpet, trombone, clarinet, tuba, piano, guitar, double bass, and drums. By the 1950s, a jazz style called Dixieland was popular in the United States and Europe. Bebop music, which began in the 1940s, became an accepted part of jazz in the 1950s. Bebop performers transformed jazz from a form of popular dance music to a faster, more experimental musical style. The most influential jazz and bebop musicians of the 1950s included saxophonist Charlie Parker, pianists Thelonius Monk and Bud Powell, trumpeters Dizzy Gillespie and Miles Davis, and drummer Max Roach. Popular bebop songs included "Groovin' High," "The Duke," and "'Round Midnight."

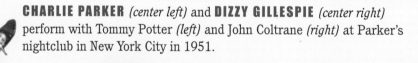

CHARLIE PARKER *(center left)* and **DIZZY GILLESPIE** *(center right)* perform with Tommy Potter *(left)* and John Coltrane *(right)* at Parker's nightclub in New York City in 1951.

■ "I WALK THE LINE": COUNTRY MUSIC

Country music combines traditional folk, Celtic, and gospel music. In the 1950s, it was often called rockabilly music. In 1956 alone, two country songs were numbers three and four on music magazine Billboard's music charts: "I Walk the Line," by Johnny Cash, and "Blue Suede Shoes," by Carl Perkins. Both men were among the most noted country artists of the era.

Beginning in the mid-1950s, a country style called Nashville Sound turned country music into a multimillion-dollar industry centered in Nashville, Tennessee. The sound brought country music to a diverse audience and made it commercially successful. Patsy Cline, Jim Reeves, and Eddy Arnold were leading artists of the Nashville Sound.

PATSY CLINE was a popular voice of the Nashville Sound.

■ "ROCK AROUND THE CLOCK": ROCK AND ROLL TAKES HOLD

A revolution, however, was brewing in the world of popular music. The younger generation was taken by storm by the introduction of rock and roll. It was a combination of rhythm and blues and country music.

Bill Haley and His Comets became one of the first groups to be labeled rock and rollers. Their "Rock Around the Clock" (1955) was a smash hit. Also in 1955, Chuck Berry blended country with rhythm and blues in "Maybellene." Berry soon was the most important black performer of early rock and roll.

Other early rock and roll musicians included Buddy Holly, Ritchie Valens, and J. P. Richardson, who was known as the Big Bopper. Holly's career lasted less than two years, coming to an end when he died in a plane crash. The singer and guitar player is remembered as one of the most influential creative forces in rock and roll. His music was sophisticated for its day because it included instruments considered unusual for rock and roll (such as a keyboard instrument called the celesta).

BILL HALEY *(center)* **AND HIS COMETS** rehearse for a performance in London in 1957.

Ritchie Valens, too, died young in a plane crash. His short career included several hits, including "La Bamba," a Mexican folk song that Valens transformed into a rock and roll hit in 1958. He is considered a pioneer of the Spanish-speaking rock-and-roll movement.

J. P. Richardson, the Big Bopper, was a disc jockey, singer, and songwriter. He had a distinctive deep voice that made him a rock and roll star. Richardson also played the guitar. "White Lightning," "Running Bear," and "Chantilly Lace" were among the songs he either wrote or performed in the 1950s. He, too, died in a plane crash—the same one that claimed the lives of Holly and Valens.

The towering idol of rock and roll was Elvis Presley. Presley was a former Memphis, Tennessee, truck driver. He wore pegged pants and had a ducktail haircut with long sideburns. Presley strummed a guitar and swiveled his hips when he sang, thrilling teenage girls and shocking their parents.

With the 1956 release of such records as "Heartbreak Hotel," "Hound Dog," and "Don't Be Cruel," Presley became an overnight sensation. "Heartbreak Hotel" was the number-one hit. "Don't Be Cruel" sold three million copies, and "Hound Dog" sold two million copies. In 1957, due largely to Presley's influence, rock and roll accounted for forty of the sixty best-selling records in the United States.

Chuck Berry is considered the most important figure in the history of rock and roll. He "melded blues, country, and a witty, defiant teen outlook into songs that influenced . . . every rock musician in his wake." The Beatles' John Lennon once said, "If you tried to give rock and roll another name, you might call it Chuck Berry."

Born in 1926 in Saint Louis, Missouri, Berry grew up singing in his church's choir. He learned to play the guitar while in high school. At first, he played a four-stringed guitar, but by 1950, he was strumming a six-stringed electric guitar. As an adult, Berry held a number of jobs, including janitor, hairdresser, photographer, and carpenter. During this time, he was also playing his guitar professionally and becoming well known around Saint Louis.

In 1955 Berry recorded "Maybellene" in Chicago. The song reached the pop charts and was number one on the rhythm and blues charts. It went on to sell more than one million copies. Berry's stage performances were known to be high-energy and fun, especially after Berry introduced his "duck walk" in 1956. The duck walk consists of jumping on one leg and moving the other in a back-and-forth motion. It looks a little like the waddle of a duck. When Berry did it while simultaneously playing the guitar, audiences went wild. Between 1957 and 1960, Berry had twenty hit

CHUCK BERRY rocks and rolls with his guitar in 1955.

songs. He was known for his unique ability to put his thoughts about subjects including love, money, fame, glory, and loneliness into song.

Berry was inducted into the Blues Foundation Hall of Fame in 1985. A year later, he was the first person ever inducted into the Rock and Roll Hall of Fame. Part of his song "Johnny B. Goode" is on board the *Voyager 1* spacecraft, an unmanned satellite that was launched in 1977 to explore the outer reaches of the solar system.

Some adults were shocked by rock and roll and offended by Presley's onstage performances. FBI director J. Edgar Hoover called rock and roll "a menace to morals." The city of Boston, Massachusetts, even banned rock concerts temporarily after several were disrupted by violent incidents. But an Arizona high school

and swing dances that were popular in the previous decades. At school dances, chaperones watched to see that students kept the proper dancing distance, which was usually about 1 foot (0.3 m). If couples danced too close, they were gently but firmly separated.

The twist was one of the most pop-

[Rock and roll is] " a menace to morals. "

—FBI director J. Edgar Hoover, 1957

student proclaimed, "Man, I believe the older generation just doesn't want the younger generation to have any fun." After Presley had appeared three times on Ed Sullivan's popular television show, Sullivan responded to the controversy by telling his audience, "I want to say to Elvis Presley and the country that this is a real decent, fine boy." Sullivan's approval of Presley did much to ease the public's concerns about rock and roll.

■ TWISTING THE NIGHT AWAY

Donning poodle skirts with petticoats and saddle shoes, dancers enjoyed more than just the waltzes

ular dances of the 1950s. Hank Ballard wrote a song called "The Twist," based on the dance he saw teenagers doing. Chubby Checker would make the song—and the dance—famous in the 1960s. The twist was the first internationally recognized dance of its kind.

The cha-cha is a Cuban dance that became popular with the Cuban music of the same name. The cha-cha beat is easy to recognize in a song: two slow beats followed by three quick ones. The steps of the dance follow the same pattern.

The stroll was an early form of line dancing. Groups of dancers stood in opposing lines facing one another,

Young people dance **THE TWIST.** The twist was one of the first dances to gain worldwide popularity.

with a wide aisle between them. The end dancers from each line proceeded from the start of the line down the middle aisle. Thus, dancers would take turns strolling down the center lane. Other popular dances in the fifties included the jitterbug, bop, the hully gully, the bunny hop, the mashed potato, the swim, and the pony.

Americans of the 1950s danced and listened to vinyl records. Large records carried a total of about a dozen songs. They were called 33s because they spun at 33⅓ revolutions per minute. Small records usually featured one song on each side. These small records were called 45s because they spun at 45 revolutions per minute. Ten 45s could be stacked onto the spindle of a record player for continuous music. (Multiple CD players of the twenty-first century use the same concept.) The 45s could be bought for as little as sixty-nine cents apiece.

Cliburn was born in Louisiana in 1934. The Cliburn family moved to Texas when Van was six. By the age of twelve, he was considered a prodigy, having won every major local piano competition. At the age of seventeen, he began studying at the world-famous Juilliard School of Music in New York City. In 1954, at the age of twenty, he debuted at Carnegie Hall, the renowned concert venue in New York City. Cliburn's performance of a composition by classical composer Pyotr Tchaikovsky was considered brilliant.

Following Cliburn's victory at the competition in Moscow, he toured in concert all over the world. Recordings of his piano performances were best sellers. During his long career, he has performed for royalty, including Queen Elizabeth II of Great Britain, and heads of state from all over the world, including every U.S. president since Harry Truman. Cliburn, who still performs throughout the United States, is dedicated to encouraging young people who are interested in being trained as classical pianists. He accomplishes this through the Van Cliburn International Piano Competition, held in Fort Worth, Texas, once every four years.

VAN CLIBURN competes in the International Tchaikovsky Piano Competition in Moscow in 1958.

Van Cliburn was hailed as a hero when he won the International Tchaikovsky Piano Competition in the Soviet Union in 1958, at the height of the Cold War. Following his victory, he was the first musician ever honored with a ticker-tape parade in New York City. Americans were grateful for Cliburn's victory, which came on the heels of the Soviets' launching of *Sputnik*.

◼ TIMELESS CLASSICS

Classical music had some important highlights in the 1950s. In 1955 Marian Anderson became the first African American singer to play a leading role at New York City's Metropolitan Opera House. That same year, *Porgy and Bess* was the first U.S. opera with African American stars to be performed at the famous La Scala Opera House in Milan, Italy.

In 1956 legendary soprano Maria Callas sang for the first time at the Metropolitan Opera in *Norma*. Her appearance grossed more than seventy-five thousand dollars, a record at that time. Also in 1956, Beverly Sills, who later became one of America's favorite opera singers, made her debut in *The Ballad of Baby Doe* in Colorado.

Twenty-three-year-old Van Cliburn won first prize at the International Tchaikovsky Piano Competition in 1958. This achievement brought him instant fame. He appeared on the cover of *Time* and was honored with a ticker-tape parade in New York City.

Aaron Copland, Leonard Bernstein, Roy Harris, and John Cage were among the decade's most prominent American composers. Many people consider Copland to be the greatest American composer of the twentieth century. Bernstein was a conductor, composer, author, pianist, and music lecturer. He composed the music for musical theater such as *West Side Story*, *Candide*, and *On the Town*. Roy Harris was the first U.S. composer to conduct his own works in Russia. John Cage was a pioneer in electronic music and in the nontraditional use of musical instruments. For example, he altered the sound of the piano by placing various objects on the strings.

MARIA CALLAS performs the title role in the opera *Norma* at the Metropolitan Opera in New York City in 1956.

New York Giants owner Horace Stoneham *(left)* and manager Leo
Durocher *(right)* hug Bobby Thomson after Thomson hit a ninth-
inning home run to beat the Brooklyn Dodgers and SEND THE
GIANTS TO THE 1951 WORLD SERIES.

Chapter Ten

AMERICA'S GAMES:
Sports and Recreation in the 1950s

With new technologies, Americans of the 1950s had more leisure time. Improved means of transportation, for example, reduced the travel time between home and work. Electric appliances allowed housewives to do chores more quickly and have more time for leisure activities. People of all ages had more time for playing and enjoying sports. But the decade's biggest change in the world of sports was television. It brought all types of sporting events into family homes. At first, promoters feared that fewer people would attend sporting events. Instead, the opposite was true. TV created more fans, who became more attracted to favorite teams and athletic heroes. These fans were willing to pay to watch their favorites play in person.

■ THE NATIONAL PASTIME: BASEBALL

Historians generally agree that baseball's greatest single game was played on August 12, 1951. On the last day of the regular season, the Brooklyn Dodgers and the New York Giants were tied for first place. For only the second time in National League history, a three-game playoff would decide the championship. The Giants won the first game. The Dodgers won the second. Everything now depended on the third game. The entire nation was caught up in the drama. Fans who didn't have TVs at home stood in the streets to watch the game on television sets in store windows. Stock reports from Wall Street were interrupted for the play-by-play account. Announcers at horse racing tracks provided more coverage of the baseball game than they did of the horse races.

Brooklyn was leading 4–2 in the last half of the ninth inning and appeared headed for victory. Two Giants were on base when tall, lanky third baseman Bobby Thomson came to the plate. On the second pitch, he hit a home run. New York won the game, 5–4, and the National League pennant. It was a thrilling end to the Giants' season.

The Giants went on to lose the World Series to the New York Yankees, but this was not surprising. The Yankees were the dominant baseball team in the 1950s. The team won eight American League pennants and six World Series that decade.

Yankee superstar Joe DiMaggio retired from baseball in 1951. He had a lifetime batting average of .325 and hit 361 home runs. He had at least one hit in fifty-six consecutive games, a record that still stands.

Mickey Mantle replaced DiMaggio in the outfield. Mantle became one of the game's most powerful sluggers. He hit 536 home runs in his career. Other outstanding Yankees in the fifties included catcher Yogi Berra; second baseman Billy Martin; and pitchers Whitey Ford and Don Larsen. In 1956 Larsen pitched the only perfect game in World Series history, allowing no hits, no walks, and no runs.

BASEBALL LEGENDS *(from left)* **TED WILLIAMS, YOGI BERRA, AND MICKEY MANTLE** pose for a picture during spring training in Florida in 1953.

HANK AARON is considered one of the most consistent players in baseball history.

Henry "Hank" Aaron was born in Mobile, Alabama, in 1934. Aaron became interested in sports at a young age and was particularly fond of baseball. After high school, he played on amateur and semipro teams. At about the same time, Jackie Robinson was breaking baseball's color barrier. In 1951, when Aaron was seventeen, he was signed to play for the Indianapolis Clowns, a team in the Negro American League. He broke into the big leagues with the Milwaukee Braves in 1954 as a right fielder.

Aaron played with the Braves for fourteen seasons. On April 8, 1974, he did what had previously been considered impossible: he broke Babe Ruth's lifetime record of 714 home runs. Throughout his career Aaron hit 755 home runs, a remarkable record that stood until 2007.

Nicknamed Hammerin' Hank, Aaron played in 3,298 games and led the majors with 2,297 runs batted in. He twice led the National League in batting and four times in home runs. He played in twenty-four All-Star games, a record he shares with Willie Mays and Stan Musial. Aaron's lifetime batting average was .305, and in his two trips to the World Series, he batted .364.

Aaron retired from baseball after the 1976 season. Shortly after, he became an executive with the Braves organization, becoming one of the first black Americans hired in a major league front office. Aaron has founded programs that encourage minorities to play major-league baseball and makes public appearances on behalf of a variety of charities. In 2002 President George W. Bush awarded him the Presidential Medal of Freedom, the nation's highest civilian honor.

Among the many non-Yankees who were great players in the 1950s were pitcher Bob Lemon of the Cleveland Indians and outfielder Stan Musial of the St. Louis Cardinals. Outfielders Ted Williams of the Boston Red Sox; "Duke" Snider of the Brooklyn Dodgers; and Al Kaline of the Detroit Tigers also thrilled their fans.

One of the most important developments in baseball was the introduction of black players into the major leagues. Jackie Robinson was the first African American to break the color barrier when the Brooklyn Dodgers signed him in 1947. During his ten-year career, Robinson batted .311, played five positions, and stole nearly two hundred bases. He achieved the ultimate honor for a baseball player in 1962, when he was inducted into the National Baseball Hall of Fame, in Cooperstown, New York.

Soon there were other outstanding black players in the major leagues. Willie Mays of the New York Giants led the National League in home runs and stolen bases for several years during the decade. Ernie Banks joined the Chicago Cubs in 1954 as a shortstop. He hit forty or more home runs five times in his career and won two league MVP (most valuable player) awards. Pitcher Don Newcombe of the Brooklyn Dodgers in 1956 won the first Cy Young Award, which honors the best major-league pitcher. Hank Aaron led the Milwaukee Braves when they defeated the New York Yankees in the 1957 World Series. Roy Campanella was another superstar for Brooklyn, both as a hitter and a catcher. In 1958 Campanella was badly injured in an automobile accident that left him partly paralyzed and confined to a wheelchair until his death in 1993.

The New York Giants and the Brooklyn Dodgers made news in another way in 1958. Both teams moved to the West Coast—the Giants to San Francisco and the Dodgers to Los Angeles. For the first time, Major League Baseball became a transcontinental sport. The Los Angeles Dodgers won the 1959 World Series against the Chicago White Sox.

■ FOOTBALL COMES TO TV

Coach Bud Wilkinson's University of Oklahoma teams dominated college football in the 1950s. From 1953 to 1957, the team won a record forty-seven games in a row.

There was no dominant professional football team in the 1950s.

The first Super Bowl would not be played until 1967. The only teams that won more than one league championship were Baltimore (two), Detroit (three), and Cleveland (three). In 1957 the Cleveland Browns acquired a remarkable fullback, Jim Brown. Brown averaged more than 5 yards (4.5 m) every time he carried the ball. He set an outstanding record by gaining 12,312 yards (11,258 m) during his nine years at Cleveland.

On December 28, 1958, the New York Giants and the Baltimore Colts met for the league championship in what sportswriter Tex Maule called "the best football game ever played." The Giants were leading, 17–14, but with only seven seconds left, the Colts' Steve Myhra kicked a field goal that tied the score.

This sent the game into overtime. Then Colts quarterback Johnny Unitas, starting on his team's 20-yard line, mixed short passes and runs to advance the ball up the field. On a successful gamble, he threw a pass to tight end Jim Mutscheller, who caught it on the Giants' 1-yard line. On the next play, fullback Alan Ameche plunged over the goal line, giving the Colts a 23–17 victory.

COLTS QUARTERBACK JOHNNY UNITAS drops back to throw a pass during sudden death overtime against the New York Giants in 1958.

This was the first championship pro football game broadcast coast-to-coast on television. It was watched by an estimated 50 million viewers. This single event, more than any other, transformed pro football into a major sports attraction. Beginning in the late 1960s, more people watched the Super Bowl than baseball's World Series.

■ RUSSELL REWRITES THE RULES

No college basketball team dominated the 1950s. During that decade, however, Kentucky won two National Collegiate Athletic Association (NCAA) championship titles. Kansas, North Carolina, and Indiana each won one.

The most sensational college basketball star in the fifties was Bill Russell. Russell played center for the University of San Francisco. He led the team to an incredible fifty-five straight victories and two national championships. Russell made such an impact on the game that the NCAA doubled the width of the lane from 6 feet (2 m) to 12 feet (4 m). This change became known as the Russell rule.

Russell played in the 1956 Olympics and led the United States team to a gold medal. That year the Boston Celtics traded two players to Saint Louis for the rights to Russell. Sportswriter Joe Jares said the trade was "probably the most important personnel deal in pro basketball's history."

In professional basketball, the two most outstanding teams in the 1950s were the Minneapolis Lakers and the Boston Celtics. Led by George Mikan, Minneapolis won three straight titles early in the decade. Most of Mikan's basketball career occurred in the 1940s, but he continued to be a dominant player through the

BILL RUSSELL *(left)* played at the University of San Francisco before leading the U.S. Olympic team and the Boston Celtics to victory in the late 1950s.

1954 season. In 1950 *Sport* magazine published the results of a poll of basketball coaches throughout the country. Mikan was named the greatest basketball player in the first half of the century.

After Mikan retired in 1954, a new professional basketball dynasty took shape in Boston. The superstars of the Celtics were Bob Cousy, Bill Sharman, Tom Heinsohn and, of course, Bill Russell. Beginning with the 1958–1959 season, the Boston Celtics won eight championships in a row.

■ TRACK-AND-FIELD STARS

In the 1952 Olympic Games at Helsinki, Finland, U.S. track-and-field athlete Bob Mathias won the decathlon (a ten-event athletic contest) for the second straight time. No other man in history had ever won the decathlon in two successive Olympic championships. Other U.S. track-and-field gold medalists in the 1952 Olympics included Lindig Rimingo (100 meters); Andy Stanfield (200 meters); Mal Whitfield (800 meters); and Harrison Dillard (110-meter hurdles).

On May 8, 1954, Parry O'Brien became the first shot-putter to throw the iron ball more than 60 feet (18 m). Traditionally, shot-putters stood at a right angle to the direction in which they would throw. But O'Brien introduced the practice of beginning with his back to the toe board. This starting position pitted the force of his weight, strength, and agility into a 180-degree turn rather than the usual mere 90 degrees. This enabled O'Brien to toss the iron ball 60 feet 5¼ inches (18 m). At the 1956 Olympics in Melbourne, Australia, he surpassed this mark, throwing 60 feet 11 inches (18.5 m) in his gold medal–winning effort.

BOB MATHIAS won two Olympic gold medals in the decathlon. This photo shows him pole-vaulting at the 1952 Olympics in Helsinki, Finland.

In these 1956 Olympics, Americans won other gold medals. Charley Dumas high-jumped 6 feet 11¼ inches (2 m). Later that year, he soared over the bar at 7 feet ½ inches (2.1 m) to set a new world record. Al Oerter tossed the discus 184 feet 11 inches (56 m). In 1962 he became the first man to throw the discus more than 200 feet (61 m).

Bobby Morrow won three gold medals in the 1956 Olympics—in the 100 meters, the 200 meters, and the 4 x 100 relay. Glen Davis ran the 400-meter hurdles in 50.1 seconds. Harold Connolly captured the hammer throw with a toss of 207 feet 3½ inches (63 m). Milton Campbell won the decathlon.

Wilma Rudolph overcame childhood polio to become a high school basketball player. She led her team to the state championship in 1955. At the age of sixteen, she earned a spot on the U.S. Olympic track-and-field team. She competed at the 1956 Olympics, where she won a bronze medal in the women's 4 x 100-meter relay.

■ "LITTLE MO" AND ALTHEA: TENNIS'S BIGGEST STARS

Pancho Gonzales was probably the best U.S. male tennis player in the 1950s, but women dominated the sport in that decade. At the age of sixteen, Maureen Connolly won the National Women's Singles Championship in 1951, becoming the youngest national tennis champion since 1901. Little Mo, as she was called, performed another remarkable feat in 1953. She became the first woman to win the grand slam of tennis. This means she captured the United States, Australian, French, and Wimbledon titles in the same year.

Althea Gibson also had a remarkable career in the fifties. Since she was African American, Gibson found it difficult to find top-notch players to compete against because only a few tournaments were open to blacks. In 1950 she became the first African American allowed to compete in the U.S. Lawn Tennis Association's national championship. That year Gibson was eliminated in the second round, but she kept trying. In 1957, at the age of thirty, she won both the United States and the Wimbledon crowns, thus ending the racial barrier in tennis. She repeated her double victory the following year.

Maureen "Little Mo" Connolly performed another remarkable feat in 1953. She became the first woman to win the grand slam of tennis.

Althea Gibson (1927–2003) paved the way for African American athletes such as tennis players Arthur Ashe and Venus and Serena Williams, and golfers such as Tiger Woods. Called the Jackie Robinson of tennis, she broke down racial barriers in both tennis and golf.

In 1947 Gibson won the first of ten consecutive national championships run by the American Tennis Association (ATA). The ATA was the governing body for black players before the sport was integrated. In 1953 Gibson graduated from Florida A&M University on a tennis and basketball scholarship. At about the same time, the color barrier in sports was broken.

ALTHEA GIBSON was the first African American player to win at Wimbledon *(above)*.

After college, integration gave Gibson the opportunity to play against the best tennis players from around the world. In 1955 she won the Italian Championship. The following year, she won the French Championship in both singles and doubles. She also became the first African American player to win at Wimbledon, when she captured the doubles crown. She reached the finals of the U.S. Championship but lost. In 1957 she won the doubles title at the Australian Championship and the first of two consecutive Wimbledon singles titles. When she returned to the United States, she was greeted with a ticker-tape parade in New York City. She went on to win the U.S. Championships, becoming the number-one-ranked player in the world. The Associated Press (AP) named her its Female Athlete of the Year in 1957. In 1958, after successfully defending her Wimbledon singles title and winning her third consecutive Wimbledon doubles title, Gibson again won the singles title at the U.S. Championship. AP named her its Female Athlete of the Year for the second time. Gibson retired from tennis that same year and was later inducted into the International Tennis Hall of Fame.

In 1964 she became the first black woman to play in the Ladies Professional Golf Association (LPGA). In her thirties by then, however, she was too old to be a champion. She played only a few years, but her efforts made it possible for other black golfers to follow her lead.

123

■ A "KING" AND A PRESIDENT LOVE GOLF

On February 2, 1949, Ben Hogan, the world's greatest golfer, was severely injured in a car accident. Doctors doubted he would ever walk normally again. They were certain he would never again play tournament golf.

Hogan, however, had unconquerable courage and determination. Seventeen months after the accident, he won his second U.S. Open tournament. In 1953 he became the first golfer to sweep the U.S. Open, the Masters, and the British Open in a single year. Golf expert Herbert Warren Wind wrote that Hogan "was not only the outstanding golfer but the outstanding athlete of the postwar decade. He was perhaps the best golfer pound-for-pound who ever lived."

Hogan continued playing golf until 1971. After he retired, Arnold Palmer became the sport's next superstar. Palmer's first major victory was the 1954 Amateur Tournament. He attained national prominence when he won the 1958 Masters tournament at the famed course at Augusta, Georgia. Nicknamed the King, Palmer captured the Masters four times during his pro career.

The nation's most famous golfer in the 1950s was not a professional player. He was Dwight D. Eisenhower, president of the United States. After Eisenhower moved into the White House, he played golf as often as he could. "People like to follow the leader," observed the operator of the public golf courses in Washington, D.C. "The papers keep talking golf. People start talking golf and then start playing it. I tell you, the President has really given the game a shot in the arm. . . . Ever since he went into the White House, all you hear is golf, golf, golf."

BEN HOGAN hits a drive from the tenth tee at the 1953 British Open.

DRIVE-INS WERE THE CRAZE in the late 1950s.

■ RECREATION, FIFTIES-STYLE

Americans found countless ways to have fun in the fifties. Besides watching television, people watched movies—from their cars. Many of the most popular theaters were drive-ins, where people parked their cars in front of a giant screen and hooked speakers onto rolled-down windows to hear the piped-in dialogue and music. At the peak of the craze in 1958, the United States had between four thousand and five thousand drive-in theaters.

Drive-in restaurants were also popular. Customers stayed in their cars and gave their orders to waiters called carhops. The carhops delivered the food to the customers, who never had to set foot in the restaurant.

■ FADS: FROM "STUFFING" TO "REC-ROOM REMBRANDTS"

A bevy of new fads reflected young people's fun-loving spirit. "Stuffing" swept across college campuses in the late 1950s. The idea was to stuff as many people as possible into a small space. At Saint Mary's College in California, twenty-two young men squeezed into a public telephone booth. In Modesto, California, the telephone company set up a booth into which thirty-two students crammed themselves. This "sport" could even be done underwater. In Fresno,

California, seven young Fresno College men each held his breath long enough to squeeze into a phone booth sunk in a swimming pool.

In 1952 Mr. Potato Head, a toy of plastic face parts that could be stuck into a real potato, reached the commercial market. It was the first toy to be advertised on television. Toy manufacturer Wham-O began mass-producing plastic flying discs called Pluto Platters in 1957. That same year, Richard Knerr, Wham-O's cofounder, added the name Frisbee to the product. Sales soared for the flying discs, which were marketed as sports equipment.

In 1958 two California toy makers learned about gym classes in Australia where youngsters exercised with bamboo hoops. The enterprising toy makers began to manufacture plastic rings and called them Hula-hoops. Within six months, U.S. girls and boys were spinning 30 million Hula-hoops. At first, kids spun the hoops around their waists. But the fad was so popular that people began spinning them around their necks, arms, legs, and ankles. Hula-hoop contests rewarded those who completed the most spins.

Painting by number became popular in the 1950s. Customers purchased canvases on which the outline of a picture was drawn. Numbers on the drawing corresponded to vials of paint that were included in the kit. For example, all the areas marked "1" were painted red. All the areas marked "2" were painted green. All the areas marked "3" were

A girl practices her **HULA-HOOP** technique.

> **"I don't know what America is coming to when thousands of people, many of them adults, are willing to be regimented into brushing paint on a jig-saw miscellany of dictated shapes. . . . Can't you rescue some of these souls—or should I say 'morons'?— before they are lost forever?"**

—*anonymous artist, lamenting the popularity of paint-by-number art, 1954*

painted blue, and so on. People with little or no artistic talent could paint their own canvases and hang them in their homes. Americans bought twelve million kits in 1952 and 1953. By 1954 more "number paintings," based on such subjects as landscapes, seascapes, and portraits of famous people, were hanging in U.S. homes than original works of art. The White House even displayed paint-by-number pictures by government officials, including FBI director J. Edgar Hoover and New York governor Nelson Rockefeller.

Many creative artists condemned this method. One concerned artist wrote, "I don't know what America is coming to when thousands of people, many of them adults, are willing to be regimented into brushing paint on a jig-saw miscellany of dictated shapes. . . . Can't you rescue

some of these souls—or should I say 'morons'?—before they are lost forever?" Nevertheless, fans of the fad, who would come to be called Rec-Room Rembrandts (after the seventeenth-century Dutch painter) were vindicated. In 2001 an exhibit called "Paint by Number: Accounting for Taste in the 1950s" opened at the National Museum of American History in Washington, D.C.

Another American classic—the Barbie doll—debuted in 1959. The creation of businesswoman Ruth Handler, Barbie was named for Handler's daughter, Barbara. Based on a German dress-up doll that Barbara had played with, Barbie first appeared at a toy show in New York City. The doll spawned its own industry, made up of Barbie's friends, clothes, and accessories. No passing fad, the doll remains popular in the 2000s.

A YOUNG COUPLE purchases appliances at a department store in 1958. The 1950s had a strong economy that enabled many people to purchase homes and fill them with goods.

A PIVOTAL PERIOD

Some historians have identified the 1950s as an era of fun and frolic, because it followed two decades of turmoil: the Depression of the thirties and World War II, during the forties. Other historians have looked at the era's pressure to conform and have called it a bland decade. Yet the fifties was neither a carefree nor a bland era. It was a decade of stark contrasts.

■ DECADE OF CONTRASTS

Americans of the 1950s enjoyed the security of prosperity under a strong economy. Jobs were secure, and many people moved to the suburbs, where they purchased their first houses, cars, and televisions. Yet the specters of Communism and the Korean War and Cold War undermined their sense of security. The hydrogen bomb, an important technological advance in the fifties, remained a danger well beyond that decade.

Writers in the fifties produced works that often reflected and sometimes critiqued society's concerns over Communism in the American government and entertainment industries. At the same time, patriotic movies and family-friendly TV shows comforted Americans who believed that the appeal of personal freedoms and a capitalist economic system eventually would defeat Communism. And indeed Soviet Communism did collapse in 1991, when the Soviet Union broke apart into independent nations.

In the 1940s, American women had entered the workforce in record numbers, replacing men who had gone overseas to fight in World War II. In the 1950s, these women had to leave their jobs, and instead, they focused on home and family. It signaled a return to a more traditional way of life but left many women feeling dissatisfied and unfulfilled. Many American women had enjoyed the independence and economic clout the war-time jobs provided. They wondered if there was more to life than cooking, cleaning, and raising children.

the rise of leaders such as Martin Luther King Jr., and the landmark desegregation decision in *Brown vs. Board of Education*—eventually came long-awaited gains in civil rights for black Americans.

As television became widespread and news programming brought more information directly into people's living rooms, the world seemed to get smaller. Exciting new developments in transportation—the U.S. highway system, faster automobiles, and jet planes—made it possible for more people to experience the world

Many American women had enjoyed the independence and economic clout the wartime jobs provided. They wondered if there was more to life than cooking, cleaning, and raising children.

Americans thrilled to the music of African American performers such as Chuck Berry and Charlie Parker. They hailed the athletic accomplishments of Willie Mays and Bill Russell. Yet black Americans remained segregated and discriminated against in U.S. society. From a long series of events in the 1950s—including Emmett Till's brutal murder, Rosa Parks's courage on a city bus,

in ways they never had before. New technologies, including Fortran, and medical breakthroughs such as penicillin and the polio vaccine, simplified and lengthened people's lives, ensuring that life in the United States would never be the same. Credit cards made purchasing goods and services easier but in subsequent decades would lead to careless spending and massive personal debt.

A U.S. Army helicopter hovers over soldiers in a combat zone in Vietnam in the early 1960s. **THE VIETNAM WAR, AS WELL AS THE PUSH FOR CIVIL RIGHTS, MADE THE 1960s A TURBULENT DECADE.**

■ WHAT HAPPENED NEXT?

The conformist 1950s gave way to the turbulent 1960s, which were marked by the escalation of the war in Vietnam and mass protests against U.S. involvement in the war. Black Americans continued the struggle for civil rights. Women, too, would demand equal rights, and many sought fulfillment by following in the footsteps of their forties forebears by working outside the home. Young women would conclude that a college education was about more than just finding a suitable husband. Boys and young men would mark their own rebellions by growing their hair long. The Beatles, a British import, would take rock and roll to new heights in the sixties. And technology would land a man on the moon in the 1960s. For all their fears and conflicts, Americans of the 1950s looked to the future with hope.

1950

- The Korean War begins when North Korea attacks South Korea.
- President Harry Truman orders production of the hydrogen bomb.
- Senator Joseph McCarthy starts his campaign to root out U.S. Communists.
- Millions of Americans begin moving to the suburbs.

1951

- General Douglas MacArthur is relieved of his command in the Korean War.
- Julius and Ethel Rosenberg are convicted of espionage. They are executed two years later.
- *I Love Lucy* and Edward R. Murrow's *See It Now* debut on television.
- Marlon Brando stars in the film *A Streetcar Named Desire*.
- Bobby Thomson's ninth-inning home run powers the New York Giants to victory over the Brooklyn Dodgers.

1952

- The United States explodes the first hydrogen bomb.
- Republican Dwight Eisenhower defeats Democrat Adlai Stevenson in the presidential election.
- Bob Mathias becomes the first man to win the decathlon in two successive Olympic Games.
- Gary Cooper stars in *High Noon*, believed by many film historians to be the best Western movie ever made.

1953

- An armistice ending the Korean War is signed at Panmunjom, North Korea.
- Marilyn Monroe becomes the decade's leading movie actress.
- Maureen Connolly wins the grand slam in tennis.
- Ben Hogan becomes the first golfer to win the U.S. Open, Masters, and British Open in the same year.

1954

- The Supreme Court decides in *Brown v. Board of Education* that segregation in public schools is unconstitutional.
- The U.S. Navy launches the *Nautilus*, the first atomic-powered submarine.
- Dr. Jonas Salk develops the polio vaccine.
- Ernest Hemingway wins the Nobel Prize in Literature for his novel *The Old Man and the Sea*.
- Shot-putter Parry O'Brien is the first man to toss the iron ball more than 60 feet (18 m).

1955

- Emmett Till is murdered in Mississippi.
- The Montgomery bus boycott begins.
- Marian Anderson is the first African American singer to play a leading role at the Metropolitan Opera in New York.
- James Dean stars in three films before dying in a car crash.
- Bill Russell leads the University of San Francisco's basketball team to fifty-five straight wins.
- Men adopt the fashion of wearing pink shirts and pink striped or polka-dot ties.

1956

- President Eisenhower wins a second term in the White House.
- The National Defense Highway Act provides for building 41,000 miles (66,000 km) of highways.
- Singer Elvis Presley becomes an overnight sensation.
- *My Fair Lady*, the biggest musical hit of the decade, opens on Broadway.
- New York Yankees pitcher Don Larsen pitches the first and so far only perfect game in World Series history.

1957

- The Soviets' *Sputnik* is the first satellite to orbit Earth.
- President Eisenhower sends troops to end segregation at Central High School in Little Rock, Arkansas.
- The musical *West Side Story* opens on Broadway.
- Jack Kerouac's *On the Road* is published, inspiring the Beat Generation.
- Althea Gibson ends the racial barrier in tennis, winning both the U.S. and Wimbledon crowns.

1958

- The United States enters the space race when *Explorer* is launched into orbit.
- Commercial jet planes are introduced.
- Hula-hoops become a national fad.
- Van Cliburn wins first place in the International Tchaikovsky Piano Competition.
- The New York Giants move to San Francisco, and the Brooklyn Dodgers move to Los Angeles.
- The Baltimore Colts' victory over the New York Giants makes pro football a major sport.

1959

- The Saint Lawrence Seaway is completed.
- Alaska and Hawaii become U.S. states.
- The television quiz show scandals are exposed.
- *The Sound of Music* is the decade's last great musical stage show.
- Frank Lloyd Wright's Guggenheim Museum opens in New York City.

SOURCE NOTES

6 Joseph C. Goulden, *The Best Years: 1945–1950* (New York: Atheneum, 1976), 19.

7 William Manchester, *The Glory and the Dream: A Narrative History of America, 1932–1972*, (Boston: Little, Brown, 1974), 653.

12 John Whiteclay Chambers II, ed., *The Oxford Companion to American Military History* (New York: Oxford University Press, 1999), 369.

12 Ibid.

12 Stuart A. Kallen, ed., *The 1950s* (San Diego: Greenhaven Press, 2000), 48.

13 David Halberstam, *The Fifties* (New York: Fawcett Columbine, 1993), 110.

15 John Toland, *In Mortal Combat: Korea, 1950–1953* (New York: Morrow, 1991), 437–438.

16 David McCullough, *Truman* (New York: Simon and Schuster, 1992), 986.

17 Douglas T. Miller and Marion Nowak, *The Fifties: The Way We Really Were* (New York: Doubleday, 1977), 27.

17 Ibid., 21.

22 Eric F. Goldman, *The Crucial Decade and After: America, 1945–1960* (New York: Random House, 1960), 141.

23 Ronald Radosh, "Case Closed: The Rosenbergs Were Soviet Spies," *Los Angeles Times*, September 17, 2008, www.latimes.com/news/opinion/la-oe-radosh17-2008sep17,0,490961.story (October 1, 2008).

24 Time-Life, *The American Dream: The 50s* (Alexandria, VA: Time-Life Books, 1998), 80.

27 Goldman, 142.

27 Lisle A. Rose, *The Cold War Comes to Main Street: America in 1950* (Lawrence: University Press of Kansas, 1999), 157.

27 Congressional Quarterly, *National Party Conventions, 1831–1992* (Washington, DC: Congressional Quarterly, 1995), 97.

27 Rose, 157.

27–28 Paul F. Boller Jr., *Presidential Campaigns*

(New York: Oxford University Press, 1984), 281.

28 Time-Life, *This Fabulous Century: 1950* (New York: Time-Life Books, 1970), 27.

28 Ibid.

32 Warren I. Cohen, *America in the Age of Soviet Power, 1945–1991* (New York: Cambridge University Press, 1993), 89.

33 Cohen, 95.

38 Academy of Achievement, "Jonas Salk Interview," *Academy of Achievement*, May 16, 1991, http://www.achievement.org/autodoc/page/sal0int=1 (October 16, 2008).

39 Ibid.

40 Harold Evans, *The American Century* (New York: Knopf, 1998), 435.

42 Miller and Nowak, 138.

45 Ray Kroc, *Grinding It Out: The Making of McDonald's* (New York: H. Regnery, 1977), 157.

46 McDonald's Corporation, "The McDonald's History," *McDonald's*, 2008, http://www.mcdonalds.com/corp/about/mcd_history_pg1.html (August 1, 2008).

46 United Airlines, "An Airplane Trip by Jet. Third Edition (1957)," YouTube, n.d., http://www.youtube.com/watch?v=sfbvFusR43k (October 10, 2008).

54 Miller and Nowak, 132.

55 Halberstam, 137.

57 Manchester, 1974, 528.

57 Time-Life, *The American Dream*, 53.

59 PBS, "The Murder of Emmett Till," *American Experience*, DVD, (Boston: WGBH Educational Foundation, 2003).

60 Manchester, 1973, 900.

61 Ibid.

61 Elizabeth Jacoway, *Turn Away Thy Son: Little Rock, the Crisis That Shocked the Nation* (New York: Free Press, 2007), 253.

68 Nash K. Burger, "Books of the Times," *New York Times*, July 16, 1951, http://partners.nytimes.com/books.98/09/13/specials/salinger-rye02.html (February 13, 2009).

68 Ian Hamilton. *In Search of J. D. Salinger* (Madison: University of Wisconsin Press, 1955), 155.

70 Jeffrey Marks, *Atomic Renaissance: Women Mystery Writers of the 1940s and 1950s* (New York: Delphi Books, 2003), 142.

71 Emily Toth, *Inside Peyton Place: The Life of Grace Metalious* (Jackson: University Press of Mississippi, 2000), 3.

72 Ibid., 239.

72 Ibid., 3.

77 Time-Life, *The American Dream*, 134.

79 Ibid.

90 Halberstam, 185.

96 Time-Life, *The American Dream*, 171.

98 Time-Life, *This Fabulous Century*, 269.

99 Ibid.

101 Richard Griffith and Arthur Mayer, *The Movies* (New York: Bonanza Books, 1957), 66.

109 D. K. Penemy, "Chuck Berry," *History of Rock*, n.d., http://www.history-of-rock .com/berry.htm (October 10, 2008).

109 Ibid.

110 Time-Life, *Rock and Roll Generation: Teen Life in the 50s* (Alexandria, VA: Time-Life Books, 1998), 44.

110 Ibid.

110 Ibid.

110 Halberstam, 479.

119 Wells Twombly, *200 Years of Sport in America: A Pageant of a Nation at Play* (New York: McGraw-Hill, 1976), 245.

120 Joe Jares, *Basketball: The American Game* (Chicago: Follett, 1971), 209.

124 Ibid., 240.

124 Edmund Lindop and Joseph Jares, *White House Sportsmen* (Boston: Houghton Mifflin, 1964), 94.

127 Dan Robbins, *Whatever Happened to Paint-By-Numbers? A Humorous Personal Account of What It Took to Make Anyone an 'Artist'* (Delavan, WI: Possum Hill Press, 1998), 317.

127 Ibid.

SELECTED BIBLIOGRAPHY

Aaron, Hank, and Lonnie Wheeler. *I Had a Hammer: The Hank Aaron Story*. New York: HarperPerennial, 2007.
Aaron's reminiscences of boyhood friends, former teammates, and baseball executives enhance this autobiography of one of baseball's greatest players.

Ambrose, Stephen. *Eisenhower: The President*. New York: Simon and Schuster, 1984.
This biography delves into Eisenhower's life and achievements. It traces his family background, education, military and political careers, and his influence as a statesman.

Antonson, Joan M., and William S. Hanable. *Alaska's Heritage*. Vol. 2. 2nd Ed. Anchorage: Alaska Historical Society, 1992.
Volume 1 summarizes Alaska's natural history and presents the human history of the land to 1867. Volume 2 covers the years since 1867.

Baughman, Judith. *American Decades: 1950–1959*. Detroit: Gale Research, 1994.
This book is an in-depth look at history, politics, law, economics, culture, and sports in America in the 1950s.

Cox, Caroline. *Stiletto*. New York: Collins Design, 2004.
Since its invention in the 1950s, the stiletto has brought sophistication and glamour—and foot problems—to women throughout the world. Cox brings her authority as a fashion historian to unravel the mystique surrounding the stiletto heel.

Dibble, Sheldon, et al. *Ka Moolelo Hawai'i* [The History of Hawai'i]. Book 3. Honolulu: University of Hawai'i Press, 2000.
This is the first Hawaiian history book written and published in Hawaii and the first from a Hawaiian point of view.

Duncan, Susan Kirsch. *Levittown: The Way We Were*. New York: Maple Hill Press, 1999.
This history of the first Levittown blends the author's personal anecdotes with facts about the Levitt family and the construction of Levittown, New York.

Kroc, Ray. *Grinding It Out: The Making of McDonald's*. New York: H. Regnery, 1977.
In an entertaining and revealing style, Kroc explains in detail how McDonald's was established. The author is unusually candid about the personal and professional challenges he encountered on his way to becoming one of America's greatest entrepreneurs.

McCullough, David. *Truman*. New York: Simon and Schuster, 1992.
This Pulitzer Prize-winning biography of Truman is a historical look at his presidency and a tribute to Truman's personal values.

Metalious, Grace. *Peyton Place*. New York: Julian Messner & Co., 1956.
The notorious, best-selling novel of 1956 follows the lives of fictional characters in a small New England town. By the early 2000s, it had sold more than 10 million copies worldwide and was the fourth-biggest-selling novel of all time.

Miller, Douglas T., and Marion Nowak. *The Fifties: The Way We Really Were*. New York: Doubleday, 1977.
This mostly pictorial look at U.S. life in the 1950s includes glimpses of the decade's evolution of fashion, motion pictures, television, and more.

Radosh, Ronald. "Case Closed: The Rosenbergs Were Soviet Spies." *Los Angeles Times*, September 17, 2008, http://www.latimes.com/news/opinion/la-oe-radosh17-2008sep17,0,490961.story. (October 1, 2008).
Radosh's in-depth article presents much of the case for and against the Rosenbergs and details Sobel's decisive 2008 confession.

Sanders, Coyne Stephen, and Tom Gilbert. *Desilu: The Story of Lucille Ball and Desi Arnaz*. New York: HarperCollins, 1993.
The first dual biography of Ball and Arnaz, this book delves into the duo's business and personal lives. Colleagues, friends, and relatives contributed to detailing the couple's successes and failures.

Strolley, Richard B., and Time-Life Books Editorial Staff. *The American Dream: The 50s*. Alexandria, VA: Time-Life Books, 1998.
Enhanced by hundreds of photographs, this book explores U.S. life, culture, entertainment, education, and more in the 1950s.

Ward, Geoffrey C., and Ken Burns. *Baseball: An Illustrated History*. New York: Knopf, 1994.
More than just a history of America's pastime, this book chronicles baseball's role in U.S. life and the way it has influenced (and been influenced by) events, trends, and customs that shaped the country.

TO LEARN MORE

Books

Darby, Jean. *Dwight D. Eisenhower*. Minneapolis: Twenty-First Century Books, 2004.
This book examines Eisenhower's life, his presidency, and his legacy.

Feldman, Ruth Tenzer. *The Korean War*. Minneapolis: Twenty-First Century Books, 2004.
Beginning with the events that led to Korea's division, this book examines the significant battles and campaigns and the negotiations that led to an armistice. Also examined are the roles that minorities and women played in the war.

Finlayson, Reggie. *We Shall Overcome: The History of the American Civil Rights Movement*. Minneapolis: Twenty-First Century Books, 2003.
Using songs, stories, and other archival material, the author tells the civil rights story from the point of view of those who lived through the movement.

Gherman, Beverly. *Anne Morrow Lindbergh: Between the Sea and the Stars*. Minneapolis: Twenty-First Century Books, 2008.
Lindbergh once wrote that her goal in life was to marry a hero. She achieved her goal but in so doing became a hero herself, achieving in fields that were uncommon for women of her time. This biography recounts Lindbergh's life, her aviation achievements, and her development as a writer.

Gourley, Catherine. *Gidgets and Women Warriors: Perceptions of Women in the 1950s and 1960s*. Minneapolis: Twenty-First Century Books, 2008.
This fascinating title examines changing views of women—from the conformist 1950s through the rebellious 1960s. Gourley looks at advertisements, popular magazines, and other media to explore how women of this time were perceived and how they perceived themselves.

Kluger, Jeffrey. *Splendid Solution: Jonas Salk and the Conquest of Polio*. New York: Putnam, 2005.
More than a biography of Salk, this book tells how polio was beaten in one of the triumphs of modern medicine.

Kuhn, Betsy. *The Race for Space: The United States and the Soviet Union Compete for the New Frontier*. Minneapolis: Twenty-First Century Books, 2006.
Using archival photos and historical quotes, Kuhn tells how Americans geared up to beat the Soviets in space. Kuhn follows the race—from *Sputnik* to the moon.

Lazo, Caroline Evensen. *Harry S. Truman*. Minneapolis: Twenty-First Century Books, 2003.
Following the death of President Roosevelt, Truman suddenly found himself thrust into the most powerful job in the world. This biography discusses Truman's early years, education, and family life, as well as his political career and post-presidential life.

Marling, Karal Ann. *As Seen on TV: The Visual Culture of Everyday Life in the 1950s*. Cambridge, MA: Harvard University Press, 1998.
This informative look at 1950s U.S. culture explores the early days of television and its influence on society. Marling also delves into the automobile's popularity, Cold War politics, and the influence of celebrities such as Elvis Presley.

Sherman, Josepha. *The Cold War*. Minneapolis: Twenty-First Century Books, 2004.
This book examines the armed conflicts and political battles during the fifty-year power struggle between the Soviet Union, the United States, and their respective allies.

Vascellaro, Charlie. *Hank Aaron: A Biography*. Westport, CT: Greenwood Press, 2005.
This biography provides a portrait of Aaron as a baseball player, as well as a man who endured racism and animosity as he chased Babe Ruth's record. Aaron's desire to excel both personally and professionally continues to inspire people young and old.

Viola, Kevin. *Joe DiMaggio*. Minneapolis: Twenty-First Century Books, 2006.
This book discusses DiMaggio's professional career and personal life as one of baseball's greatest players.

Films

The Big Picture: Fifty Years of Aviation. DVD. Washington, DC: National Archives and Records Administration, 2008.
This documentary examines the extraordinary accomplishment of flight and details the advances that have occurred in the first half of the twentieth century.

Korea: The Forgotten War. DVD. New York City: A&E Home Video, 2005.
This compelling documentary from the History Channel tells the story of the Korean conflict. It includes interviews with combat veterans, film clips from the war's key battles, photographs, and more.

Sputnik Mania. DVD. Directed by David Hoffman. Santa Cruz, CA: Varied Directions International, 2007.

This award-winning documentary was produced to celebrate the fiftieth anniversary of *Sputnik*'s launch and how the little satellite changed the world. It tells the story of *Sputnik* from America's point of view.

Websites

The Dwight D. Eisenhower Presidential Library and Museum
http://www.eisenhower.archives.gov
President Dwight D. Eisenhower was a critical part of the 1950s. This site offers everything related to the president's life—from a detailed biography to photos to speeches to a tour through the museum's exhibits.

Korean War Veterans Memorial
http://www.nps.gov/kwvm
This memorial was dedicated in 1995 to honor the U.S. men and women who served in the war and those who gave their lives for the cause of freedom. It includes in-depth information about the war, the memorial, and activities.

Little Rock Central High School National Historic Site
http://www.nps.gov.chsc
Explore the events surrounding the integration of Little Rock's Central High School in 1957. This site includes photos, interviews, resources, and an online tour of the school.

SELECTED 1950s CLASSICS

Books

Hemingway, Ernest. *The Old Man and the Sea*. 1952. Reprint, New York: Bloom's Literary Criticism, 2008.
Hemingway's classic tale of a fisherman who goes head-to-head with a marlin encapsulates the author's favorite themes of physical and moral challenges.

Peale, Norman Vincent. *The Power of Positive Thinking*. 1955. Reprint, New York: Fireside, 2007.
Long before *The Secret*, this revered classic taught millions of readers to achieve personal fulfillment through the power of faith in action.

Salinger, J. D. *The Catcher in the Rye*. 1956. Reprint, New York: Back Bay Books, 2001.
Sixteen-year-old Holden Caulfield narrates the events that occur for two days following his expulsion from prep school.

Films

Ben-Hur. DVD. Directed by William Wyler. Burbank, CA: Warner Home Video, 1959. Charlton Heston stars as Jewish prince Judah Ben-Hur, who is found guilty of an attempted murder that he did not commit. Enslaved on a warship, Ben-Hur escapes and seeks to exact revenge on his powerful enemy by competing against him in the Roman chariot races. This is filmmaking on a scale that had never been seen before.

High Noon. DVD. Directed by Fred Zinnemann. Hollywood, CA: Republic Pictures, 1952. Gary Cooper stars as newlywed sheriff Will Kane. His plans to settle down with his wife, played by Grace Kelly, are interrupted when he learns that gunslinger Frank Miller is headed into town at high noon to settle an old score. Kane seeks the assistance of deputies and townsfolk, but soon realizes he'll have to stand alone in his showdown with Miller.

Invasion of the Body Snatchers. DVD. Directed by Don Siegel. Hollywood, CA: Republic Pictures, 1956. Kevin McCarthy portrays Dr. Miles Bennell, who doesn't believe his neighbors and patients when they tell him their loved ones are acting strangely. But soon Bennell realizes that his town has been invaded by alien pods that replicate humans and take possession of their identities. Bennell risks his life to battle against the alien invasion.

s ACTIVITY

Identify six to ten things that relate to the 1950s. (To start your thinking, consider your parents' and grandparents' lives, family antiques or collections, houses or buildings in your neighborhood, favorite movies, books, songs, or TV shows, or places you've visited.) Use photographs, mementos, and words to create a print or computer scrapbook of your 1950s connections.

141

ABOUT THE AUTHOR

Based in California, Edmund Lindop wrote several books for the Presidents Who Dared series as well as several of the titles in The Decades of Twentieth-Century America series.

Sarah DeCapua was born in Connecticut and graduated from Springfield College (BS) and Sacred Heart University (MAT). She is an editor and author for young readers. She lives in suburban Atlanta.

PHOTO ACKNOWLEDGMENTS